CHURCH

WHERE ARE YOU?

CHURCH

WHERE ARE YOU?

RECOGNIZE A HIRELING – REVEAL A WOLF – REVIVE A CITY

INCUBATION

ANGELA D. TANNER

Printed in the United States of America
First Printing, 2010
ISBN 978-1-941749-59-3
Library of Congress Catalog Number 201612354
4-P Publishing
Chattanooga, TN 37411

Cover design by Kingdom Graphica

First Edition: September 2016

CONTENTS

DEDICATION

To my Heavenly Father, my true best friend. You keep me laughing! Out loud! Powerful and mighty! You Reign!

To my Mom, One amazing woman! Thank you for your tender love and care. Your wisdom and gentleness, taught me to strive for a pure heart, deep within. I will see you again, my beautiful, heavenly sent mother, and very best of friends. I miss you.

To my Children, you are amazing. I laughed just writing that! Truly, truly amazing. Our love is unbelievable. You are unbelievable. My joy, Kanisa, Natisha, Khari, Jeremy, Lamarr.

To my additional son, Sammy, Son you are incredible, kind and too funny. I cherish our relationship. Jesus is here! I love you.

– 'Moms'

Special Dedication

To Silverdale Correctional Institution and Hamilton County Jail, Chattanooga, Tn. "Rise up!" We're here, for your fight. Don't miss this amazing life! Jesus is no joke! You've got to represent, though. Be doers of the word, that you read and hear. For you, it's been made clear. "You are Never Forgotten and Never Alone." – We are Heaven's messengers, sent out to lift you, through love. Now, it's time to stand up!

To Broad River Rd. Correctional Facilities, West Columbia, S.C., where, Mom taught the GED and literacy program, at Kirkland. Be strong. Stray from wrong. Amazing her love for you, her earnest heart to teach you. God's heart is calling you. Choose this day, whom you will serve. God, has already, chosen you. – Choose Me

To Chicago, Philadelphia, Atlanta and Los Angeles, where I was born and lived, as a child and N.Y. Hear, God's call on your life. He's waking soldiers up, in the night, in prayer, for your fight. Cities, stand! A Mighty God, is reaching, His hand. Though, the 'church', may not have yet, come for you - it's time to choose. - Jesus Christ is coming back, soon. He is coming, for you. Get ready. Judgement starts in the house of God. It is starting, now. Make Jesus Christ, your everlasting life. – Choose Me.

To the Jails across America, God is with you. You are not a disappointment, but the very beat, of God's Heart. The world's got it wrong. The church, has leaders, leading wrong. Wake up, in Jesus Christ and be strong! You are never, alone. "And lo, I am with you always, even unto the end of the world." – Jesus. - Choose Me

To the Housing Centers all around the Country, to struggling parents and heart broken families, tears flowing through your eyes. God is your prize, through your Lord and Savior, Jesus Christ. He'll walk beside you. You will know, He is there. You will feel Him in the atmosphere. He will make your day! He will make you laugh, as you walk, talk and pray. He paves a holy, loving path, of miraculous ways. He is here for you. A consumed fire, giving you, your heart's desire. Delight yourself, fully in Him – Jesus Christ, Son of the Living God – A way maker - I Am. – Choose Me.

To the Chattanooga Police Dept., Red Bank Police Dept. and all of our loyal Police Departments throughout America and the world. Our love and gratitude for you, as we, the 'Community Church" take serious, our instructions from the Lord, to reach into our own neighborhoods with community service. We support you by; Opening our 'closed' doors, to reach out to our youth, embracing them at a very early age, as we visit homes and personally bring the children, to our 'daily open' doors, at our church facility. We pray, unceasingly for you. From the very depths of our heart,

Thank you! "Obligated Blue, (Chapter 10) -We love you."

INTRODUCTION

If, God's people, are not involved in, 'wicked ways', why does God say 'we' are? If, we say we are not, a part of wickedness, then are we calling God a liar? Is God a liar, now?

Do we, corporately announce to church members, or friends, to come to church? After all, the scripture says, "We should not forsake the assembly of meeting together, with one another." Right? So, why do we settle for going to and joining church organizations that do not, go to the prisons? Doesn't the word of God say, "…When you visit the prisoner, you visit me." And "…depart from me, when I was in prison, you did not visit me." Sounds pretty serious, doesn't it? Yet, do we have prison ministries, at our church facilities? Do we actively, go and see, "Jesus?"

The word of God says to, "Go into the highways and hedges and compel others to come…" Highways and hedges, are the main roads, the side roads and country lanes. We put a 'Welcome' sign out front, with a famous quote or scripture and this is 'our' invitation. We put up signs and make announcements in our pulpits, yet the word of God says, to "Go and compel", go and urge others, persuade them, to come. Do we go into the neighborhoods?

The scriptures say, "We will do the work Christ did and even greater works shall we do." Is anyone questioning where these, "Works of Christ and greater works" are, in our local ministries?

The Word says, "…When I was a stranger, you took me in…" Also, "…depart from me, when I was a stranger you did *not* take me in…" So, the church facilities, are closed all week, nice beautiful building, closed, and the homeless are all around the city, hungry, cold, hot, and dirty. So, the church facility is created for, "Jesus." Right? Yet, Jesus says, He is the stranger, the homeless, the hurting, the drug addict, the prostitute, the very least of these. (Mat. 25:35-46). We, pick and choose what scriptures matter the 'most', don't we?

In his book, *Evangelism That Works,* Author George Barna, says, "The most unused structures in the country, are church facilities."

… *So, are we, involved in, "wicked" yet?*

"The Early Church did not alone support missionaries; it was missionary."
- *"An audacity of faith. These men actually expected to convert the world."*
Helen Barrett Montgomery, The Bible and Missions

Local Leaders, leading sheep astray

I was watching the local news, recently. A reporter, asked a well-known pastor, with one of the largest church facilities in the city, "What needs to be done about the gang violence, which has resulted in several homicides?" He answered, "The people, in the neighborhood, need to start taking care of each other."
In other words; the housing development centers (low income and poverty stricken area) and surrounding streets, filled with a large portion of the city's crime, gang violence, fathers and youth in prison, drug dealings, killings, Mothers distraught with their young sons already in a grave, some, have two sons gone, families full of despair and heartache, --now these devastated and hopeless, broken families, needing themselves to come up for air and breathe, need to start taking care of one another.

Isn't that what Jesus assigned the 'Church" to do? Doesn't He say, "The harvest is plentiful, but the workers are few, pray then to the Lord of the harvest, for workers to 'go into' His harvest fields?" (Mat. 9:37) Has not Jesus told us, "the church", to go into the highways and hedges, into the streets? (Luke 14:23). Doesn't He say, for the strong to bear the infirmities of the weak? (Rom. 15:1)
"Who executes justice for the oppressed…?" (Ps. 146:8)
"…those who close their eyes to poverty will be cursed…" (Pro. 28:27)

Are we involved in, "wicked" yet?

How many families in our local congregations, have foster children or have adopted? You, would think the pastors would be teaching this, since after all, Jesus, their employer, says to care for the orphans. (James 1:27). Yet, our city and states are in desperate need of foster parents. Especially, good, wholesome, loving parents. Is your church family, willing to take in an orphan, or is your own home available, to 'take a stranger in?" (Mat. 25:35).
Our leaders, are leading the sheep, away from Christ, but you decide. You better, decide quickly, because if we continue, our 'church going' life, as though the church has no wicked inside, woe to our land, our cities, our communities, our own lives…
An old African Proverb says…
"It's not a wise man who goes to sleep with his neighbor's house on fire."
Our Cities are burning, with our children inside

CHURCH WHERE ARE YOU?

The *Real* Church is Our Only Hope, for the City!

"If my people, who are called by my name, will humble themselves and pray and seek my face and turn from their wicked ways, then I will hear from heaven, and I will forgive their sins and will heal their land."
 (2 Chron. 7:14)

Often, we are 'stuck', with *not* assessing, where the local church, truly is, because we have been falsely taught, and believe, we are *not* to judge. However, the 'truth' is,
 we are *not* to judge the world, but we *are* to 'judge' the church...

"For what have I to do with judging outsiders? Is it not those inside the church whom you are to judge? (1 Cor. 5:12)

"Do not judge by appearances, but judge with right judgement."
 (John 7:24)

As pulpits across the country are filled with teaching, to "find your purpose', and seemingly every 'spiritual' book, now on the shelf is teaching the same, I ask you, "What has happened, to God's purpose?" (Luke 19:10)

The streets are empty of 'the church's' presence and the neighborhood children,
 youth and their families, are void of our concern.

CHURCH WHERE ARE YOU?

In the following pages, I present to you, Our Cities are dying, along with our youth and elderly, in the hands of hirelings, preachers for pay. (John 10:13)

Recognize a hireling, a wolf in disguise, break away and begin
The true work of Jesus Christ...
Save your city
Your youth, your children, your elderly, your family. (Jude 1:23)
 "For it is time for judgement to begin with God's household" (1 Pet. 4:17)
 (John 12:46-48)

Chapter One

RUDE AWAKENING

HIRELING
HEAT LAMPS
FOR SALE
$5

He That Wins Souls is Wise

Ministries are closed!
Open your eyes
Open two days a week
Paying, a hireling
Even, if the pastor
Has, a second job
Trying to excuse, "I have a job"
This, does *not* excuse
What Jesus told us to do
With a secular job, the pastor can delegate
But then, he'd have to share his pay
And you don't think, he knows this
If, he has another job
And this one, is just for God
Why, isn't he doing what God says
Why, is he and everyone acting confused?
Our instructions are clear. Jesus says, go!
And He, will add the souls. This means, organize
He that wins souls is wise. Satan is killing our kids
How can we continue to live, indoors, in our worship facilities?
We are at war. Faith without works, is dead. Is your church doing, as Jesus said
Praying for the streets. And not going to the streets, is no strategy. It's dead
Jesus says, it's dead faith. Satan's strategy is to destroy. We're still taught
Like little girls and boys. Me, Me, Me. What about Me?
Please feed me. More, more, more mysteries
What's your Church's strategy
Will, pastors share their salary
To equip, teach, train and go
Go set the neighborhoods free!
Write the vision, make it plain…
By the way, when is baptism for new souls
In the Name of the Father, Son and Holy Ghost
When is baptism scheduled, in Jesus Name…

> "*The Harvest
> is plentiful
> the **workers**
> are few.*"
>
> (*Luke 10:2*)

**Are you 100% sure…
your leader is not, now seeking personal gain?**

"He that wins souls is wise..." (Pro. 11:30)

"So you see, faith by itself isn't enough. Unless it produces good deeds, it is dead and useless."
(James 2:17)

"...And the Lord added to their number day by day those who were being saved." (Acts 2:47)

"The thief comes only to steal and kill and destroy...."
(John 10:10)

"...Go out to the highways and hedges and compel men to come in, that my house will be full." (Luke 14:23)

"...Write down the revelation and make it plain..." (Hab. 2:2)

"The hired hand runs away because he's working only for the money and doesn't really care about the sheep."
(John 10:13)

Prayer;

_____

_____

_____

_____

_____

_____

_____

_____

_____

_____

_____

Love Your Neighbor, as Yourself

Jesus, makes His plan very clear
The fruit, of God's spirit, is very real
We need patience, with prayer in our life
But, if we don't begin, to do what is right
We're soon, gonna' die, and leave this life
Don't leave here, with your work undone
Jesus commanded, that lost hearts be won
Stop seeking, "the churched only" members
What about, the addict and the gang member
Leaders, have a lot of deep, teaching going on
So why, are we yet so weak and still not strong
Why? Because we need works, with our faith
We're to be doers of the word, not hearers only
Our entire mission, is clear. Surrounded around
Winning the lost. Loving, interacting with others
We, are passionately concerned, for one another
We are united, blood bought, sisters and brothers
As a result, the community knows us, by our love
Why, does Jesus want the world, to know us, this way
So, He can use us, to win them, to Him. With love and kindness
Have I drawn thee. We take our love, between one another, place it
With His plan and His love stands. Jesus' love, bears up under anything
No devil, no curse, greater than He with us. Write the vision for soul winning
And go! This will also, strengthen families within. Gets families involved, in
Helping others. Turning love outward, not in
Love others, as you love yourself. Caring about 'your own' world, is NOT
What Jesus told us to do. Satan has stolen the word. When this is what we do
We strengthen our lives, by being a part of, each other's pain and hurt…

**This is how we bring healing
To the lost and to the church**

"Some people are like seed along the path, where the word is sown. As soon as they hear it, Satan comes and takes away the word that was sown in them." (Mark 4:15)

"...Love your neighbor as yourself."
(Mat. 29:39)

"But just don't listen to God's word. You must do what it says. Otherwise, you are only fooling yourself." (James 1:22)

"The fruit of the righteous is a tree of life, and whoever captures souls is wise." (Pro. 11:30)

*"Rejoice with those who rejoice; weep with those who weep. Live in harmony with one another. Do not be haughty, **but associate with the lowly**. Never be wise in your own sight."*
(Rom. 12:15-16)

"Remember those in prison as though bound with them..."
(Heb. 13:3)

Prayer;

_____

_____

_____

_____

_____

_____

_____

_____

_____

_____

God, Make Us a Family...To Go

> "Keep on loving one another as brothers and sisters."
> (Heb. 13:1)

Isn't God's family, amazing
Most everyone, loves family
And whether family is around or not
We, make our friends, become family
God gives us, one another, as family
He makes us, brothers and sisters
It's part of God's purpose
His plan, to make us Fam
All, that is horrible, turns fine, when we follow His design
He builds our family, an extended family tree
It's so much fun, with new hearts won
Hanging out. No fear, no loneliness, no doubt
Working toward, a much greater life
Laying hands on the sick, casting out evil spirits
The lame walk. The deaf hear and talk
The blind see. His plan for you and me
What do you mean, "If it's His will?"
Hasn't He told us His will? To win the lost
We Advertise, "God and I are friends"
So why, do we not, know Him

> "Do the work of an evangelist."
> (2 Tim. 4:5)

God, gave each of us, gifts. To fulfill **His** purpose
And His purpose for us, is to serve, as He served
To reach the lost, He sent His Son, to pay the cost
It's like working at Chick-Fil-a. Each worker, has an assignment
Yet, the main goal...Is to, with honor, serve the greatest chicken sandwich
As a family, we have allowed an enemy, to confuse us, about our main goal
Digging a deeper hole. Leaders focusing attention, on finding 'our' purpose

Our purpose has already been told. Cultivate our gifts, as we...

GO

!

"...Go out to the highways and hedges and compel people to come, so that my house will be full." (Luke 14:23)

"No longer do I call you servants, for a servant does not know what his master is doing; but I have called you friends, for all that I have heard from my Father I have made known to you." (John 15:15)

"they will pick up serpents with their hands; and if they drink any deadly poison, it will not hurt them; they will lay hands on the sick, and they will recover." (Mark 16:18)

"...whoever believes in Me will also do the works I do; and greater works than these will he do, because I am going to the Father." (John 14:12)

"Therefore go and make disciples of all nations, baptizing them in the name of the Father, and of the Son and of the Holy Spirit, and teaching them to obey everything I have commanded you. And surely I am with you always, to the very end of the age." (Mat. 28:19-20)

Prayer;

_____

_____

_____

_____

_____

_____

_____

_____

_____

Go and Win My Lost

We, take time for one another
Always praying for each other
Our common ground, is not the particular job we do
Our common ground, is God greatly using me and you
Using us each, to build His Kingdom
To grow His family, here on earth
How hard, would we be working
If we knew, time was running out
Our children, our parents, our friends
Our neighbors, our co-workers
Were about to spend eternity
Never dying, burning and crying
Would outreach, be an emergency
Well, this is what, is happening

> *"The student is not above the teacher, but everyone who is fully trained will be like their teacher."*
> *(Luke 6:40)*

God, is sending back His Son, to Rapture all that have been won
We're still sittin' in the pews, talkin' 'bout, "What to do, what to do?"
Truth is, we are ignoring, what to do
The student has become, greater than the teacher
Shepherds and sheep, are the student. Jesus is the teacher
The students, are no longer listening to, or following the teacher
Why, do we 'act' confused. God himself says, we know what to do
My sheep know MY voice. A stranger, they will not follow. They will FLEE!!!
Jesus says, stop excusing and following shepherds, that are not following Me!
Write a plan and go to the street. If the local church, truly has Me, where are…
My Newly Redeemed? Where, are the lost sheep, those that are being saved
After…I redeemed you? I came for the sick, not the righteous
My lost sheep are My main focus. Why isn't it yours?
My Father, will not even send Me back
My child, for you, without them too
My harvest Is plenty!
I love you…

I am your Father and I know you are not confused
But, you follow leaders, who refuse
To go to my lost sheep

CHURCH WHERE ARE YOU?

*"But you will receive power when the Holy Spirit comes upon you. And you will be my witnesses, telling people **about me** everywhere ...to the ends of the earth" (Acts 1:8)*

"...many false prophets will arise and lead many astray."
(Mat. 24:11)

"It will happen, in a moment, in the blink of an eye, when the last trumpet is blown. For when the trumpet sounds, those who have died will be raised to live forever. And we who are living will also be transformed." (1 Cor. 5:15:52)

"The son of man will send out his angels, and they will weed out of his kingdom everything that causes sin and all who do evil. They will throw them into the blazing furnace, where there will be weeping and gnashing of teeth."
(Mat. 13:42)

Prayer;

_____
_____
_____
_____
_____
_____
_____
_____
_____
_____
_____
_____
_____
_____
_____
_____

And Even Greater Works Will We Do

When, will we realize, it's our teaching
It's been watered down and compromised
The Deeper, more mysterious the mysteries
Still, we are drawn away, from our true calling
We are called, fishers of men. What is the problem?
We are serving under hirelings, preachers for pay
They fly to preach in different cities
Because, their eye is on that penny!
We, can't serve God and money
Yet, you still, walk among them
Jesus says, do not partner with them
It appears hard for us, to be convinced
Not really. We know, we aren't satisfied
Jesus is trying to give us, Our Father's eyes
This is why, we visit from church to church
Finally settling on, the good, the bad, the worse
Married to Christ, yet the wife is not in her own bed
She has gone astray, not knowing her husband, her true head
Why is God's bride, so hard to find? Why does she stay in and hide?
We're lost in our own family. Who's responsible? The wolves and hirelings
How can we hear, without a preacher? And how can he preach, except he be sent
Satan has sent wolves, in our mist. Hirelings for pay, are his. Sent to confuse us
These are not God's servants. They open churches, for a dollar
On Sunday, they preach, teach, they may holler
But because, we refuse to study our bible
Satan has blinded us and stolen revival
You don't have to take it from me
When, has the local church's
greater works been seen
Where is the integrity
To go win the lost?

Jesus says, I will make you fishers of men
Where are the others, you are winning to Him?
When is baptism?

"...My harvest is plentiful, my laborers are few." (Mat. 9:37)

"...whoever believes in me will do the works I have been doing, and they will do even greater things than these..." (John 14:12)

"...No immoral, impure or greedy person...has any inheritance in the Kingdom of Christ and of God." (Eph. 5:5)

"Therefore do not be partners with them." (Eph. 5:7)

"If I have the gift of prophesy and can fathom all mysteries and all knowledge, and I have faith that can move mountains, but do not have love, I am nothing." (1 Cor. 13:2)

"And how can anyone preach unless they are sent? As it is written: 'How beautiful are the feet of those who bring good news!'" (Rom. 10:15)

*"Consequently, faith comes from hearing the message, and the message is heard **through the word about Christ.**" (Rom. 10:17)*

"Beware of false prophets, who come disguised as harmless sheep but are really vicious wolves."
(Mat. 7:15)

Prayer;

_____

_____

_____

_____

_____

_____

Satan Believes and Trembles

Come, let us reason together
Can you understand, how frantic Satan is
The bible says, he believes and he trembles
Now, what would make anyone that scared
To shake and become, frightened in terror
Satan knows, the mighty power of God
The creator of the entire universe
He has seen, the Red Sea split
He has seen, the plagues of Egypt
He has seen, the boils and open sores on Job
And yet, Job continued to sing praises to God
Satan knows, if we ever get a hold of Christ like this
It's over for him! He knows Samson, killed the philistines
He was there, inside King Saul, as a boy trusted his Lord God
This boy, David, killed Goliath, and an army fell into his hands
Satan knows, with three hundred soldiers, Gideon killed thousands
And, when God opened, Elijah's servant's eyes, he saw Horses
On Chariots of fire! Satan knows, whenever God wants
He will speak through a donkey or a burning bush
Satan devised leprosy, disease, to be placed on men
They meet Jesus, and they are made whole again
Satan is trembling, scared and frightened
When God is given, the full hearts of men
The paralyzed walk. The lame, grow limbs
And those that are lost, are born again
Satan has seen many deaf, sing praise
When we go out, into the highways
Men, are going to turn to God's ways
Satan knows, God's Word is true
So he strategies, to keep it from you
Jesus says, BEWARE OF WOLVES!

Satan trembles, when we walk in truth
If you really have Me, you can deliver the City
Why is My Church, scared to go to the 'plenty'?

"Come now, let us reason together..." (Is. 1:18)

"You say you have faith, for you believe that there is one God. Good for you! Even the demons believe this, and they tremble in terror." (James 2:19)

"Then the angel of the LORD appeared to him in flames of fire from within a bush. Moses saw that though the bush was on fire it did not burn up." (Ex. 3:2)

"Reaching into his shepherd's bag and taking out a stone, he hurled it with his sling and hit the philistine on his forehead. The stone sank in, and Goliath stumbled and fell face down on the ground." (1 Sam. 17:49)

"And Elisha prayed, 'Open his eyes, Lord, so that he may see.' Then the LORD opened the servant's eyes, and he looked and saw the hills full of horses and chariots of fire all around Elisha.'" (2 Kings 6:17)

"...Go out to the roads and country lanes and compel them to come in, so that my house will be full." (Luke 14:23)

Prayer;

_____

_____

_____

_____

_____

_____

_____

_____

Try the Spirit and See if it is of God

We know, what we can each do, individually
One, can send, a thousand demons to flight
Together, two can send, ten thousand to flight
So, Satan definitely, does not want us to unite
He strategizes. To pull the 'wolf' over our eyes
We are serving, under hirelings and wolves
"Try the spirit and see if it is of God."
They WILL NOT take us to the prison
They WILL NOT take us to the hood
They WILL NOT take us to the hungry
They WILL NOT take us to the street
They WILL NOT teach us to adopt the orphaned
Or care for the fatherless, widows or foster children
They WILL NOT unite us, with sisters and brothers
In other ministries, for us to go into the neighborhoods
Who do you think they serve? The answer is themselves
The wolves just WILL NOT, Go! Not to the poor homes
The hireling's church, is not going to help, save the city
The hireling's church, has no written plan to win the gangs
No days mapped out, to go out regularly, into the community
Are you kidding me? To the crack houses, to pray with the addicts?
No way! Satan doesn't want, the lost souls set free, from addiction
The wolves, can only offer excuses for why their church doesn't go
Their agenda, is entirely different from
The Mat. 25:35 and Luke 23:14 outreach
"He that gives to the poor, lends to the Lord"
Not the hireling church. You will be shockingly
Surprised at what this ministry, honestly gives
Satan has this world, hurting, dying and in tears
Wolves livin' on that income, while the hood lives in fear
The local church, the world sees no help, and no answer here
The real church, is the ANSWER, to All, of this world's mess
But, God's children, still in the pews, looking…clueless

**Who will flee, from the wolves and hirelings
Who will go spread My word and heal the community?
Only, God's Spirit can go, and pray and set sinners, free**

"...I am afraid that as the serpent deceived Eve by his cunning, your thoughts will be led astray from a sincere and pure devotion to Christ." (2 Cor. 11:3)

"You happily put up with whatever anyone tells you, even if they preach a different Jesus than the one we preach, or a different kind of Spirit than the one you received, or a different kind of gospel than the one you believed."
(2 Cor. 11:4)

"I am astonished that you are so quickly deserting the one who called you to live in the grace of Christ and are turning to a different gospel- which is really no gospel at all. Evidently some people are throwing you into confusion and are trying to pervert the gospel of Christ." (Gal. 1:6-7)

"Beloved, do not believe every spirit, but test the spirit to see whether they are from God, for MANY false prophets have gone out into the world."
(1 John 4:1)

Prayer;

_____
_____
_____
_____
_____
_____
_____
_____
_____
_____

Lion of Judah

Sheep expose wolves
But, aren't sheep dumb
No! That's another one
Another, of Satan's lies
Dumb prey, in his eyes
Truthfully, we are
Wise, as serpents
Gentle, as doves
We soar, like eagles
Spreading God's love
We're holy and meek
We Follow like sheep
When a wolf shows up
There's a LION in me
The Lion of Judah
I'm cub to the King
Wolves don't scare me
I, don't follow wolves
Wolves, leading sheep
Now that's weak
They teach bible stories
Mix lies with God's glory
They, have learned well
To suppress, any people
Hide from them, who they really are
So the local church, has lost her power. Listening to a liar
Jesus said, Run… FLEE! Run from the liar and return to Me
Your hands are anointed. Heal the sick and to raise the dead
Go and cast out evil, and do all I've said
My anointing breaks yokes.
MY POWER NO JOKE!
But, you, treatin' Me
Like Imma' hoax…

> "For the kingdom of God is not a matter of talk but of power."
> (1 Cor. 4:20)

> "Those whom I love, I reprove and discipline, so be zealous and repent."
> (Rev. 3:19)

Yeah, you treatin' Me, like I'm a joke. I set captives, FREE!
Wake up! From your misery! I'm the REAL thing!
King of Kings! Lord of Everything!

"…If you knew the gift God has for you and who you are speaking to, you would ask me, and I would give you living water." (John 4:10)

"The Spirit of the Lord is upon me, because he has anointed me to proclaim good news to the poor. He has sent me to proclaim freedom for the prisoners and recovery of sight for the blind, to set the oppressed free." (Luke 4:18)

"For I resolved to know nothing while I was with you except Jesus Christ and him crucified." (1Cor. 2:2)

"… I am sending you out as sheep in the midst of wolves, so be wise as serpents and innocent as doves." (Mat. 10:16)

"But those who hope in the LORD will renew their strength. They will soar high on wings like eagles…" (Is. 40:31)

"…Stop weeping! Look, the Lion of the tribe of Judah, the heir to David's throne, has won the victory…" (Rev. 5:5)

"I am the good shepherd; I know my sheep and my sheep know me- just as the Father knows me and I know the Father- and I lay down my life for the sheep."
(John 10:14-15)

Prayer;

_____

_____

_____

_____

_____

_____

Pastor, We Need the Truth - I

The messages, that I've heard
Have made me, ponder and wonder
Are the pastors running out, of words?
Is it, just your voice, you want heard?
Why, are you adding, to God's word?
Is it just you, we hear? Is Jesus, near?
It's HIS word only, that sets captives free
Please, do not ever, begin to teach without HE
We've been listening, watching you, a while
But, walking with Jesus, sweeter along the miles
Every minute is new. I can't wake up, to just you
For this life, I lived here, only Jesus, will ever do
Miraculous, in my life. My holy, living sacrifice
Got me, constantly excited. My Father, is always there
I can't run out of HIS words. God's love is unconditional
I don't want, 'me' to be heard. Father, speak Your words
I can't breathe without You. I can't see without You
I can't live without You. Even, for one more moment
Jesus, please, please for me, give the preachers, a word
Now on TV, the preacher is preaching. He says, "When you say, I love you
You need to tell your family why." He says, "Cause, anyone can say, I love you
So, you need to tell your spouse why. Tell your kids why. Why, do I love you.?"
He says, "Because you take care of the bills. And, you take care of the children
And, you do this, and I do that." Sorry preacher. Preacher, that's not why I love
I love because, I was first loved. I love because, of this amazing, anointed love
It's impossible, to keep it to myself. Even when I try. It's a love I cannot hide
It's a consumed fire, burning my desire. Jeremiah says, it's like fire shut up
In my bones! I pray for you Preacher, that you stop speaking on your own
God is a consumed fire. I can't keep THIS Love to myself, even if I tried
He has lit my heart with fire! Preacher, you got to seek…'His' desire
Pastor, cry out to Jesus Christ for the city, and tell God's children
The Truth. If you don't, very soon, you may be removed…

Will Jesus have to make the rocks cry, out for you?

"Beloved, if God so loved us, we ought to love one another."
(1 John 4:11)

"This is the message you have heard from the beginning: We should love one another."
(1 John 3:11)

"A new commandment I give you: Love one another. As I have loved you, so you must love one another." (John 13:4)

"Be devoted to one another in love. Honor one another above yourselves." (Rom. 12:10)

"If I have the gift of prophesy and can fathom all mysteries and all knowledge, and if I have a faith that can move mountains, but do not have love, I am nothing." (1 Cor. 13:2)

"Whoever does not love does not know God, because God is love."
(1 John 4:8)

Jesus help me to love like You, not according to what others do, or don't do
Jesus make me speak, only Your truth. Jesus, let me lean, only on You
Please Lord, let my mouth, preach only Your truths
Jesus, let me die and live only through You

Prayer;

_____

_____

_____

_____

_____

_____

_____

_____

Pastor, We Need the Truth – II

So the preacher says, there needs to be
A reason, I love you. He gave a few examples;
"Family members, need to be told, 'why' you love them
Think of things they 'do', then say, I love you"
Preacher, you are preaching your words
That's not, what needs to be heard
Why, would you pass out commands
That are clearly straight from man?
These are not, Jesus' words;
Leaders of God, this is absurd
STOP! preaching your own words
Family, I love you, despite ourselves
It's Jesus' love, that's been our never-ending help
He makes me love you, as He. He makes me love you, as me
His incredible plan, His incredible life, has my heart, burning inside
I don't love you, because you are perfect
I don't love you, because you make, no mistakes
I don't love you, because you make good grades. Baby, I love you anyway
If I say I love you, because you're strong, what happens when you're weak
If I say I love you, because you clean the house, what happens when, you don't
If I say I love you, because, you make up the bed, what happens, when you won't
If I say I love you, because you birthed, and are now raising, five beautiful kids
What happens, when there is a car accident and four of your baby girls don't live
True story. What happens then? Preacher, I'm yelling and screaming at you. Tell
The truth. STOP giving your personal, point of view. Please, tell God's children
The truth. Preacher, I love you! You got to tell God's word true. God's love…
Is unconditional. It may not be enough for you. But that doesn't matter
It's the truth. God's love is unconditional. It's from above
That's what makes it, God's Love…

Check the words, the preachers say
With God's Holy word, on the Bible's page
He's coming back, for you. And He has warned
Beware of wolves

"I am writing to remind you, dear friends, that we should love one another. This is not a new command but one we have had from the beginning. I ask that we love one another." (2 John 1:5)

"By this everyone will know that you are my disciples, if you love one another." (John 13:35)

"No one has ever seen God; if we love one another, God abides in us and his love is perfected in us."
(1 John 4:12)

"...For whoever does not love their brother and sister, whom they have seen, cannot love God, whom they have not seen."
(1 John 4:20)

"Love is patient, love is kind. It does not envy, it does not boast, it is not proud. It does not dishonor others, it is not self-seeking, it is not easily angered, it keeps no record of wrongs. Love does not delight in evil but rejoices with the truth." (1 Cor. 13:4-6)

"...love one another as I have loved you..."
(John 15:12)

Prayer;

_____

_____

_____

_____

_____

_____

_____

Chapter Two

INTRODUCTION TO HIRELINGS

You are Called, by 'My' Name

In my twenties, I sure thought the Lord was gonna' use me
Then I joined the church and they sure did abuse me
Tell me why, most everyone is so confused
Jesus has told the leaders, and all of us what to do
Why do you think the leaders, keep only, 'certain' instructions?
Do this. Do that. Do not forsake, coming together to church to meet
But, they don't really care, if you go to the highways, to the street
Because they are hirelings, And the street offers, no offering
If you have a better answer, Satan has simply blinded you
Satan's job, is to pull the wool over your eyes
Tell me, is there another reason why
If offerings were taken, in the prisons and housing projects
How many of these assignments, would the pastor reject?
The answer is none. They would be preaching, we are as one
But take away the money, and people get funny
Why, is meeting at the church, all we got
Why, are we not listening to God
The sinners are out here, in this world
Satan, is in the street, killing our boys and girls
Since we won't go into his territory, he has no fear of us
So, he comes right into the church house, and deceives us
It's a hard truth, but it's the truth. Pastor's aren't going to God's lost sheep
If he tells you, he is not to go, he's lying. Do the work, of an Evangelist
And fulfill your ministry. Isn't that instruction for he, you and me?
That's what shepherd's do, they physically, lead sheep
So why aren't the pastors going. Why aren't they leading?
Because the church is content. And will not flee, from a hireling
Neither does the church care, that they are not, going anywhere
We like to dress up, learn new mysteries, and sit in the pews
It's what, the wolves and hirelings have gotten us, use to
A form of godliness, denying God's real power
The church is the answer, for the street, this hour…

If my people, called by my name, would act like they've been changed
I will hear from heaven and I will heal their land
Jesus says, Church STAND!

"If my people who are called by my name humble themselves, and pray and seek my face and turn from their wicked ways, then I will hear from heaven and will forgive their sin and will heal their land." (2 Chron. 7:14)

"But mark this: There will be terrible times in the last days. People will be lovers of themselves, lovers of money, boastful, proud, abusive, disobedient to their parents, ungrateful, unholy." (2 Tim 3:2)

"As for you, always be sober-minded, endure suffering, do the work of an evangelist, fulfill your ministry."
(2 Tim. 4:5)

"...for it is written: 'Be holy, because I am holy.'" (1 Pet. 1:16)

"...Go out to the highways and hedges and compel them to come in..." (Luke 14:23)

"...I was sick and in prison and you didn't visit me."
(Mat. 25:43)

Prayer;

_____
_____
_____
_____
_____
_____
_____
_____
_____
_____
_____
_____
_____
_____

Woe to the Shepherds...

The greatest Dad, I ever had
Lives in Heaven, I call Him Dad
Sitting on the right hand of the throne
Stronger than strong, I'm never alone
He's amazing. Truly amazing
He's a breath of fresh air
An exhilarating heart beat
All power, in His hand
Because we're His children
Sons and daughters, we stand!
I've gone through, so very much
Often, my own doing, not His touch
Still, He redeemed me, every time
From the pain, I held deep inside
How, my heart, bled and cried
Choices, that were not wise
He, has separated, now
The pain from my heart
Kept it, just far enough apart
For me to live and tell, 'a life', story,
And decades later, still give Him glory
Back in the day, I remember, others would say
"There's no pain, like the pain you receive in church"
And I would think, "How can anyone, 'Be in church' and hurt?"
Then I joined, a Church of God in Christ, and had my heart ripped out
Right before my eyes. So happy, loving and carefree. Never knew
What was in store for me. I, can no longer, blame anybody
I chose, who I would marry. But it doesn't stop there
When you find out, your pastor, really doesn't care
Going to church, stumbling upon all his affairs
"Ain't no hurt, like the one, from church"...

> "'Woe to the shepherds who are destroying and scattering the sheep of my pasture!' Declares the LORD."
>
> (Jere. 23:1)

"Woe to the shepherds, who destroy and scatter My sheep..."
Wake up church, you are definitely...
sleep. -Jesus

"For the leaders of the people have misled them. They have led them down the path of destruction."
(Is. 9:16)

"What sorrow awaits the leaders of my people -the shepherds of my sheep- for they have destroyed and scattered the very ones they were expected to care for, says the Lord." (Jere. 23:1)

"It would be better for them to be thrown into the sea with a millstone tied around their neck than to cause one of these little ones to stumble." (Luke 17:2)

"Beware of false prophets who come disguised as harmless sheep but are really vicious wolves." (Mat. 7:15)

"God will judge those on the outside; but the scriptures say, 'You must remove the evil person from among you.'"
(1 Cor. 5:13)

"Not everyone who calls out to me, 'Lord! Lord!' will enter the Kingdom of Heaven. Only those who actually do the will of my Father in heaven will enter."
(Mat. 7:21)

Prayer;

_____
_____
_____
_____
_____
_____
_____
_____
_____
_____
_____

Leaders are Held to a Higher Standard - I

I had a friend once
Sister twice
Pretty as could be
Sweet Missionary
Married with kids
A family, did live
She came to church
A little hurt
Said, her husband
Gave her no attention
We, went to a store
Got a few things
Made her laugh
To me, family
Was everything
She counselled
With, our Pastor
That was a disaster
She fell for him
He planned
The whole thing
I tried to tell her
It was the devil
She didn't listen
They began an affair
Families died right there
I couldn't tell her, names of others
Others were, my sisters too. I told them all, he doesn't love you
Now your family is gone. His family is gone. You hurt your spouse
Violated God's house. Hurt my family. My family gone too...

> *"You were taught, with reguard to your former way of life, to put off your old self, which is being corrupted by its deceitful desires; to be made new in the attitude of your minds; and to put on the new self, created to be like God in true righteousness and holiness.*
> *(Eph. 4:22-24)*

Leaders are held to a higher standard

"What shall we say, then? Shall we go on sinning so that grace may increase? By no means! We are those who have died to sin; how can we live in it any longer?"
(Rom. 6:2)

"...among you there must not be even a hint of sexual immorality, or of any kind of impurity, or of greed, because these are improper for God's holy people." (Eph. 5:3)

"Dear brothers and sisters, not many of you should become teachers in the church, for we who teach will be judged more strictly." (James 3:1)

"The devil comes to steal, kill and destroy..." (John 10:10)

"For I am afraid that when I come I won't like what I find, and you won't like my response. I am afraid that I will find quarreling, jealousy, anger, selfishness, slander, gossip, arrogance, and disorderly behavior."
(2 Cor. 12:20)

Prayer;

_____
_____
_____
_____
_____
_____
_____
_____
_____
_____

Leaders are Held to a Higher Standard - II

Leader has no faith
Doesn't care
Broke up families
Everywhere
Decades later
Still doesn't care
Her mind is gone
She was a jewel
But now, his tool
Programmed robot
Totally forgot
Who she was, in Christ
Everyone lost so much
Alone, broken homes
Still, she wants him
It's a reprobate mind
To want his kind
Gone is your mind
Two decades later
Still waiting
To be his bride
He still got others
It's his kind
Like a zebra
Can't change stripes
He can't change
How he bites
His sharp teeth
Into you they sink
He is a wolf. You are a sheep
He turned you out. Now you're asleep
Deceived the wife. Deceived your life. Hurt your sister's
Hurt your brothers. I told you, he had others…

> "Since they thought it foolish to acknowledge God, he abandoned them to their foolish thinking and let them do the things that should never be done."
> (Rom. 1:28)

> "But she who is self-indulgent is dead while she lives."
> (1 Tim. 5:6)

Leaders are held to a higher standard

"Dear friends, do not believe every spirit, but test the spirits to see whether they are from God, because many false prophets have gone out into the world."
(1 John 4:1)

"For these are false apostles. They are deceitful workers who disguise themselves as apostles of Christ." (2 Cor. 11:13)

"I know that after I leave, savage wolves will come in among you and will not spare the flock." (Acts 20:29)

"...and many false prophets will arise and mislead many."
(Mat. 24:11)

"Watch out for false prophets. They come to you in sheep's clothing, but inwardly they are ferocious wolves."
(Mat. 7:15)

Prayer;

_____

_____

_____

_____

_____

_____

_____

_____

_____

_____

_____

_____

_____

_____

Do Not Do, as They Do

Can, you feel me
Can you heal me
When my heart kneels
I pray hard. I need to be
Near. Right, where you are
I see you. I feel you. I cry too
Jesus says, worship Him in spirit
It's real, we kneel, we feel
When my family hurts, I hurt
When my family cries, I cry
When our son dies on the street
I kneel and wail out, desperately
You are my family, for you I hurt
I am my Father's child. I am the Church!
I know this love, because, my Father loves
I'm in need. I passionately need, to talk to you
Many of these leaders, preachers, just ain't true
They're deceiving you. You got to read your bible
Your heart needs revival. That's the only truth
Can't you see, Satan destroying our youth
Can't you see, leaders, just talkin' smooth
When, will we realize…
It's not what they say
It's what they do
Jesus Christ says, these hirelings, don't care about you
So, they may not smoke or drink. And they dress perfectly
Can't you think! THEY AIN'T OUT HERE IN THESE STREETS!
Are you kidding me! Satan is our enemy. He's out there, killing in those streets
With gang life, drug life, prostitution and HIV. Wreaking havoc on the family
Pastor home, watchin' TV. His church, got zero prison ministry
But, he all up in that 'other side of town' community
Are you kidding me! Don't be deceived……
Start a real ministry…

> *"And many false prophets will appear and deceive many people." (Mat. 24:11)*

Do as they say, but not as they do
Turn lives around in the hood
That's what Jesus would do

*"So practice and obey whatever they tell you, but **don't follow their example.** For they don't practice what they teach."*
(Mat. 23:3)

"The thief comes only to steal and kill and destroy. I have come that you may have life and have it abundantly."
(John 10:10)

"And the master said to the servant, 'Go out to the highways and hedges and compel people to come in, that my house may be filled.'" (Luke 14:23)

"When did we ever see you sick and in prison and visit you? '...when you did it for one of the least of these my brothers and sisters, you were doing it for me!'" (Mat. 25:39-40)

"Rejoice with those who rejoice; mourn with those who mourn."
(Rom. 12:15)

Prayer;

_____
_____
_____
_____
_____
_____
_____
_____
_____
_____
_____
_____
_____
_____
_____
_____

Arise and Awake, Oh Sleeper

Church, you're killin' me, in your sleep
You killin' us, because you are, asleep
The pastor, is opening the church
A few hours a week, passing
The homeless, on the street
Jesus says, "That is Me!"
My "church" facility, empty
Locked up. Closed five days a week
Why, are the homeless, on the street?
Believe, you are killin' you. You, killin' me
Check to see, if your facility, feeds the hungry
Does your church have a 'full of food,' food pantry?
How does your church, use funds to feed the hungry?
Send them, to the food bank, only?
Why not bring, the hungry people
To, the great place with the steeple
So God's people, can encourage them
Get to know them and pray with them
Take them in, love on them and become friends
Eventually, bring them in. Compelled, by the love we have for them
No, let's send them to the area food bank, only. That's what it's there for
Here's your voucher, bye, shut the door. That's not enough! We need to interact
You need to recognize, these hirelings. There is enough of you, in the neighborhood
To care for one another. You're a fool, if you don't think, we're sisters and brothers
You got a prophet in your home. Stop leaving Jesus alone. Get your bible, pray for
revival. Haven't you heard, there's power in God's word
You have access to, so much power!
Satan, ain't nothing, but a coward...

"...Go out... and urge anyone you find to come..."

(Luke 14:23)

Jesus Christ...Show the one reading this
Your real life

"...Wake up, sleeper, rise from the dead and Christ will shine on you." (Eph. 5:14)

"...he gave His instructions to Israel. So the generation to come might know them...and they in turn would teach their own children. So each generation should set its hope anew on God, not forgetting his glorious miracles and obeying his commands. Then they will not be like their ancestors- stubborn, rebellious, and unfaithful, refusing to give their hearts to God."
(Ps. 78:5-8)

"In the last days, God says, 'I will pour out my spirit upon all people. Your sons and daughters will prophesy. Your young men will see visions, and your old men will dream dreams.'"
(Acts. 2:17)

"For I was hungry and you gave me something to eat, I was thirsty and you gave me something to drink, I was a stranger and you invited me in, I needed clothes and you clothed me, I was sick and you looked after me, I was in prison and you came to visit me." (Mat. 25:35-36)

Prayer;

_____
_____
_____
_____
_____
_____
_____
_____
_____
_____
_____

A Stranger They Will Not Follow

Defending wrong,
Will hurt the weak and the strong
If this is what we choose, we lose
Jesus says, rescue and defend the poor
Jesus does not tell us, the poor we have with us always
So we can relax from helping, or defend why we do nothing
If, we were not to take care of the poor, why does Jesus say
He who cares for the poor, lends to the Lord
If someone asks for 'that', give him 'this' also
Yes, it is God's instruction, to work
And we, are to carry out all of Christ instructions
Are we Not, making a difference, at the 'State Housing' Sites
Because most, may not be working. Well, God says, "Do not murder."
But, who is directed, to go to the prison and visit "murderers"
Do we not do our part, because of their personal situations
Our life is built, on Christ' heart's desire, to reach the lost!
Yes, we support and teach the instructions of Christ
But, we DO NOT leave the street to themselves
Leaders are assigned **to equip the saints, for work in ministry**
When, does the hands on training begin, for witnessing to the lost
Does middle, or high school, last a lifetime
Who, has the church, so confused
It is clear, what Jesus said to do
We contend with 'church service' 2 days a week
Never going to the street. Who is teaching the sheep?
Are we following strangers? Jesus says, "My sheep know
My voice. And a stranger, they will not follow, but will flee."
We are only to follow those, who follow obediently after Thee
We are to reach the lost, disciple them and teach them to reach
We know we are unsettled in church. And they offer us an excuse
But Jesus words, always true…

> **"They Travel over land and sea**
> **to make one disciple and turn him into**
> **twice as much a child of Satan as they are."**

"Woe to you, teachers of the law and Pharisees, you hypocrites! You travel over land and sea to win a single convert, and when you have succeeded, you make them twice as much a child of hell as you are." (Mat. 23:15)

"Defend the weak and the Fatherless; uphold the cause of the poor and the oppressed." (Ps. 82:3)

"...Remember those in prison as if you were together with them in prison, and those who are mistreated as if you yourselves were suffering." (Heb. 13:3)

"Give to anyone who asks you, and if anyone takes what belongs to you, do not demand it back." (Luke 6:30)

"For the needy will not always be forgotten." (Psalm 9:9)

"My sheep know My voice; I know them, and they follow Me." (John 10:27)

"...and the sheep follow Him, for they know His voice. A stranger they will not follow, but they will flee from Him because they don't know his voice." (John 10:4-5)

Prayer;

_____
_____
_____
_____
_____
_____
_____
_____

Recognize a Hireling

Spot a hireling, a mile away
Get close to Christ and pray
Ask Him, for His revelation
When, you read, His word
It's not hidden, from you
God takes time, to share His news
These hirelings, don't seem all bad
Could seem to be a leader, of good
But, listen carefully, guard your ears
Deep mysteries, you will hear
You will not hear much of Me
Or, how I came to set you free
I don't mean, if they're at work
And they can't mix state and church
I mean, while working in church work
They have no idea, how to set you free
Listen and see. There is little talk, of Me
There's not one thing you need, I can't do
I commanded My church, to bring Me to you
I cry in My heart, how relaxed they are
I'm coming back, for My church
Without a spot or wrinkle
Washed and cleansed
Sparkle and sprinkle
Filled with My Spirit
Walk down the street
Witness of Me, set captives free
A hireling's biggest clue, is a hireling won't come to you
They refuse to set captives free. They have been, too occupied
With their own agenda and greed. I've commanded; set captives free
Visit the prisoners, feed the hungry. Go to the highways…
This is how you serve, Me…

> "The hired hand
> is not
> the shepherd…"
>
> (John 10:12)

> "Guard your heart
> above all else, for it
> determines the
> course of your life."
> (Pro. 4:23)

Will, you come to Me
Recognize a hireling…Flee

"...I praise you Father, Lord of heaven and earth, because you have hidden these things from the wise and learned, and ...revealed them to little children." (Mat. 11:25)

"Your hands made me and formed me; give me understanding to learn your commands." (Ps. 119:73)

"There is another serious problem I have seen under the sun. Hoarding riches harms the saver."
(Eccl. 5:13)

"For such people are not serving our Lord Christ, but their own appetites. By smooth talk and flattery they deceive the minds of naïve people." (Rom. 16:18)

"...the overseer must be above reproach, the husband of but one wife, temperate, self-controlled, respectable, hospitable, able to teach, not given to drunkenness, not violent but gentle, not quarrelsome...not a lover of money." (1 Tim. 3:2-3)

"...He has sent me to proclaim deliverance to the captives."
(Luke 4:18)

"the blind see, the lame walk, the lepers are cured, the deaf hear, the dead are raised and the Good news is being preached to the poor." (Mat. 11:5)

Prayer;

_____
_____
_____
_____
_____
_____

Why, are you Not Coming to Me?

Hurting for lost souls
My children won't go
Pray then for laborers
To go, to My harvest
I have begged, you so
I need My lost, you know
But still, you will not go!
Cause the leaders are not
Physically leading you there
These days, leaders don't care
Many, are lovers of themselves
This generation, will have to guide
My sons and daughters will prophesy
If My church doesn't go, sinners will die
John the Baptist prophesized of my coming
Now, I need My church, to begin to summon
Summon My lost to Me. Set the captives free
Lay hands on the sick, and they shall be healed
Cast out demons, raise the dead. Do All I've said!
Do, the work of an evangelist and fulfill your ministry
Go and get My lost sheep. I've been begging you, a while
But, you are still on milk, My child. You have abandoned My mission
The main mission, is your assignment. As you graduate, levels in My word
You are to make sure, the lost have heard. The preachers are keeping everyone in
Not fully developing you, within. Still feeding you low fat milk, got you all
Into yourself. When will you begin, to love others as yourself
My word says, to cast your cares on Me
The cares of this world
Are keeping you
From Me…

My word says, to love others through Me
I am in the neighborhood outreach and prison ministry
I am the Fatherless, the orphaned, the streets of poverty…
Why are you not, coming to…Me?

"The harvest is plentiful, but the workers are few. Ask the Lord of the harvest, therefore, to send out workers into his harvest field. Go! I am sending you out like lambs among wolves."
(Luke 10:2-3)

"...keep your head in all situations, endure hardships, do the work of an evangelist, discharge all the duties of your ministry." (2 Tim, 4:5)

"The Lord is not slow with you, keeping his promise, as some understand slowness. Instead he is patient with you, not wanting anyone to perish, but everyone to come to repentance." (2 Pet. 3:9)

"Go into the highways and byways and compel others to come in..." (Luke 14:23)

Prayer;

_____
_____
_____
_____
_____
_____
_____
_____
_____
_____
_____
_____
_____
_____
_____
_____

Chapter Three

INCUBATING
HIRELINGS

Be a Doer, Not a Hearer Only

What, do I do if I believe, my pastor is a hireling
Well, read your word! Jesus says to, "Flee!"
He says, **"You're going to have to start**
Trusting Me! I have more for you
Then your eyes, have ever seen
Or your thoughts, have thought
I will be with, a 'Going' Church
Going, to the prisons and the hurt
Go and do the things you've heard
Read! My word tells you what to do
A workman rightly dividing My truth
I'll speak to you and I'll teach you, too
But, what you read, you must also do
This is why the preachers aren't true
They hear, but they do NOT, also do
I said, go to the prisons, will you go?
I give you My anointing, will you go?
Go to the projects, start a mission
With the elderly, the lost, the kids
Do what I say, so you can, live
A hearer and doer of My word
Get out of that dead church
Go and love and do My work
Fast, pray and read everyday
I'll be with you. Write the vision
Recruit disciples, I will lead you
I'm going to make you, fishers of men
Stand in the gap for lost souls. Share my word when you go
Go out and compel others to come in. Remember Acts 2:47
Study my word, do as you've heard
Go to the highways…
To the street…

> *"And he said to them,*
> *'Follow me, and I will*
> *make you*
> *fishers of men.'"*
> *(Mat. 4:19)*

> *"…And each day the Lord*
> *added to*
> *their fellowship those who*
> *were being saved."*
>
> *(Acts 2:47)*

"Don't get caught up in, 'busy'
And Forget about, Me. I said, Go!
Go to the highway. This is My way."
- Jesus

"Do not merely listen to the word, and so deceive yourselves. Do what it says." (James 1:22)

"Go into the highways and hedges and compel people to come in..." (Luke 14:23)

"...and the sheep follow him, for they know his voice. A stranger they will not follow, but they will flee from him, for they do not know the voice of strangers." (John 10:4-5)

"...No eye has seen, no ear has heard, and no mind has imagined what God has prepared for those who love him." (1 Cor. 2:9)

"Do your best to present yourself to God as one approved, a worker who has no need to be ashamed, rightly handling the word of truth." (2 Tim. 2:15)

"But the advocate, the Holy Spirit, whom the Father will send in my name, he will teach you all things and will remind you of everything I have told you." (John 14:26)

Prayer;

_____
_____
_____
_____
_____
_____
_____
_____
_____
_____
_____

Natural Before the Spiritual

I was listening to the local radio station
The topic was neighborhood outreach
A mom, called in and made a suggestion
She said, "An outdoor activity, at the church
Would be nice with a huge jumping apparatus."
Then a preacher called in,
He says, "People are tired of gimmicks
They want real, they want substance
The blow up jumper is not the answer."
I could have screamed
To a mom in a van with kids, on a hot day
A blow up apparatus, is not just, 'the answer'
It may be the only Answer
It may even save a life, her life or the kids life
It may save a community member's life
As you embrace this family and win them to Christ
Jesus is the Answer, the way, the truth and the life
His love is powerful. His love is life changing
A blow up apparatus, outside
With hotdogs, popcorn and drink
May be just what a hurting soul needs
Jesus teaches, the natural before the spiritual
Why do we, want to do different, from Jesus
The Teacher who has taught us
The Leader who, first leads us
He is the only good shepherd
The pastors are the under shepherds
A day of laughter, relationship building
Face painting, cold drinks and popsicles
It may, be just what the doctor ordered…

> "The fruit
> of the righteous
> is a tree of life,
> and whoever
> captures souls is
> wise."
> (Pro.11:30)

If we do not follow Jesus, closely
We will follow strangers, falsely

"But it is not the spiritual that is first but the natural, and then the spiritual." (1 Cor. 15:46)

"A cheerful heart is good medicine, but a broken spirit dries up the bones." (Pro. 17:22)

"Direct your children onto a right path, and when they are older, they will not leave it." (Pro. 22:6)

"And let the peace that comes from Christ rule in your hearts..." (Col. 3:15)

"They worshipped together at the temple each day, met in homes for the Lord's supper, and shared their meals with great joy and generosity, all the while praising God and enjoying the goodwill of all people. And each day the Lord added to their fellowship those who were being saved." (Acts 2:46)

"A stranger they will not follow, but they will flee from him, for they do not know the voice of strangers." (John 10:5)

Prayer;

_____
_____
_____
_____
_____
_____
_____
_____
_____
_____

The Hireling's Church

The hireling's church will not save the city
Stop depending on her, ridiculous pity
She, stays in doors. Hiding, like a whore
Pimped by a pimp. No leader, but a wimp
The real church, believes wholeheartedly
I, Jesus Christ, Am the Son, of the LIVING God
Taking over the City, the streets, the block
This church is built, on Me, the solid rock
This church, will individually study My word
And get My desire to the streets, to be heard
I said, "Go into the highways and byways…"
I am Jesus! Remember My words, My ways?
Lay hands, on the sick. Raise the dead. Pray!
You're telling everyone, that you work for Me
But, you work for greed, paid a corrupt fee
I said, "Go and Compel others to come to Me."
Yet, you stay in and say, I call you friend
You, My friend? Why haven't you, gone?
The sick, the lost, I have already won
You live your own agenda, and leave mine undone…
You, do not bring My lost to Me
I told you, the harvest is plenty
The gates of hell shall not prevail
Against My church, My real work
Many preachers, are killing My sheep
The church is the reason for the lost, in the city
Staying in, locking your doors, hiding like a whore
Where is My, Beautiful, Holy, Anointed and Powerful Bride
For whom I came and suffered and died? Why, won't you come outside?
Why do you compromise? Your leaders lie. My Father waits patiently to send Me
I warned you, there are wolves in disguise. Do, you seriously believe, I can't save
The city? You say, you know Me. You boast, I never change
But you forget, when Elijah prayed, I made it rain...

> "The harvest is plentiful, but the workers are few. Ask the Lord of the harvest, therefore, **to send out workers** into his harvest field.
>
> (Luke 10:2)

**…With Me
You are the hope for the city
The harvest is plenty!**

64

"…I know your works. You have a reputation that you are alive, but you are dead." (Rev. 3:1)

"Behold, I have given you authority to tread on serpents and scorpions, and over all the power of the enemy, and nothing shall hurt you." (Luke 10:19)

"Jesus came and told his disciples, 'I have been given all authority in heaven and on earth. Therefore, go and make disciples of all nations, baptizing them in the name of the Father and the Son and the Holy Spirit.'"
(Mat. 28:19)

"I tell you the truth, anyone who believes in me will do the same works I have done, and even greater works, because I am going to the Father." (John 4:12)

"Heal the sick, raise the dead, cleanse the lepers, drive out demons. You received without paying; give without pay."
(Mat.10:8)

"…they will lay hands on the sick, and they will recover."
(Mark 16:18)

Prayer;

_____
_____
_____
_____
_____
_____
_____
_____
_____
_____
_____

You Cannot Serve God and Money

Everyone is trying to find answers
Who's, gonna' tell the complete truth
Why, is the local church not thriving
Whatever, Our Father told us to do
We are not doing
All these church, 'growth' books
Somebody, please tell the truth
We're so puzzled, baffled. Why?
We got a bible. Where's revival
We're doing, what we want
His word is very clear
But, we just act confused
So, let the bible help you
Where is our Prison Ministry?
If, when we went, we got paid
Would we go to the prison weekly?
You know the answer. Yes, we would
Would we go, to the poorest homes
And mentor hundreds of young men
If, every time we went, we received
A thousand dollars, from each of them?
Let me answer for you. Yes, we would!
Would we go, to the elderly homes
And lay hands on the sick
If every time we went
We got, paid for it? Let me answer. Yes, we would!
Would we go, to the streets. And knock on twenty doors a day
Bless their homes and show the way. Teach them to believe and to pray
If every day we went, we got paid. Do I need to answer for you? You know the truth.
God knows the truth. We're not doing what He said…

> "Let each
> of you look
> not only to
> his own
> interests,
> but also
> to the
> interest of
> others."
>
> (Phil. 2:4)

Cause money has us dead
Somebody needs to tell the truth
- This is the Truth

> *"No one can serve two masters. Either you will hate the one and love the other, or you will be devoted to the one and despise the other. You cannot serve both God and money."*
>
> *(Mat. 6:24)*

Prayer;

_____
_____
_____
_____
_____
_____
_____
_____

No Longer Shall the Shepherds 'Feed On' Sheep (Ez. 34:10)

You can put you picture on the bus stop bench
You can put your picture, on the city bus
But until you come out here, to see us
It's Just your picture, on a bus
You and your beautiful wife
On a billboard, on a flier
Until you come out here
You're, perceived as a liar
You think, none of us know, the word?
We have family, aunties, uncles and cousins
You 'ain't' suppose, to stay inside, that church
With, all these people, out here dying and hurt
Even we, know this, so we know, you know this
Pastor, you doing, the basics to what gets you paid
Even the best of you, no longer coming our way
You've become hirelings, a shepherd for pay
More concentrated on the car you drive
Then whether we, are dead or alive
Yeah, you must have lost that power
You, should watch who you hang with
You know all these Pastor's don't love us
You know how they talk, when not around us
You think our life, is just some big, famous joke
Getting' rich off the city. I got news for you though
Woe. "Woe to the pastor, who scatters God's sheep"
Wake up Pastor, from that deep sleep. You've lost that power
The church knows it. You know it too. They, just lazily following you
That's what sheep do. We out here, on this street, steady crying and dying
You scared, to take a dare, so you leave all the sinners, out there. Lost and alone
-- Our family and friends in jail, you leave them all for hell, even though, God said
GO!
God please send Your laborers! God, please raise up a generation, of laborers for us!
A generation that will Go, to the highways and byways and bring us into
Your ways...
Please Lord, send Your real laborers, for us!
Thank you, Lord!

> "The hired hand is not the shepherd and does not own the sheep..."
> (John 10:12)

> "...Go out to the highways and hedges and compel people to come in, so that my house will be full."
> (Luke 14:23)

"...'Go quickly into the streets and alleys of the town and invite the poor, the crippled, the blind, and the lame.'
After the servant had done this, he reported, 'There is still room for more.' So the master said, 'Go out into the country lanes and behind the hedges and urge anyone you find to come, so that the house will be full.'" (Luke 14:21-23)

"As I live, declares the Lord GOD, surely because my sheep have become a prey, and my sheep have become food for all the wild beasts, since there was no shepherd, **and because my shepherds have not searched for my sheep, but the shepherds have fed themselves,** *and have not fed my sheep, therefore, you shepherds hear the word of the LORD: Thus says the Lord God, behold, I am against the shepherds, and I will require my sheep at their hand and put a stop to their feeding the sheep.* **No longer shall the shepherds feed themselves. I will rescue my sheep from their mouths, that they may not be food for them."** (Ez. 34:8-10)

"For I was hungry and you gave me food, I was thirsty and you gave me drink, I was a stranger and you welcomed me, I needed clothes and you clothed me, I was sick and you looked after me, I was in prison, and you visited me." ...Jesus
(Mat. 25:35-36)

Prayer;

_____
_____
_____
_____
_____
_____
_____
_____
_____

The Streets, the Poor, the Prisons

Pastors, can you get a van or a bus…

And pick fifty neighborhood kids up

Twice a week, feed them and teach?

This is love, teaching and discipleship

How are we contributing, to the youth?

If you only teach, the kids, of the church members

You are teaching these children, to be just like you

Teaching them not to reach, their own peer group

Yet, their own peers, are dying in gang violence

Why won't you impact, the city for Christ

There's no problem with you, receiving pay

But it should be because, you do things, God's way

To the prisons, visiting the lowly, settin' captives free

Jesus, told you to go out, and urge others to come in

He even gave you, how to reach them. Feed the hungry

Give drink to the thirsty. How many, would eat a hot dog

And lemonade on a hot summer day? Let's go out and COMPEL

Reach, into their homes, with visits and prayer

This is Jesus' command, to take Him there. He that wins souls is wise

Where is the wisdom, of all the years? Reading His word, yet, you fear

If Jesus says, the harvest in plenty, where are the plenty?

Where, are your new sheep? Where are the sick and elderly?

That you laid hands on, and they got well?

Now, they're coming to church, with their story, to tell

Where are the poor, you are giving to? Why does everyone in your mist

Look like you? Are there no homeless, in your city? Are there no Prisons?

So when the ex-convicts get out, they will come, to check you out

Honestly, where are the ones, that are lowly and weak?

Where are the gang members? Where are the lost sheep?

How many sinners came to church today? How many did you bring?

Pastor, you are following a different way. We are all, to reach, as Jesus said

There's no, 'exception to the rule' shed on you. If you say there is, it is not

God's truth. We are directed, to bring the lost, the weak, the sinners to Him

We are co-workers with Christ, to save the lost. This is, each of our cost

No matter, if you are an apostle, pastor, evangelist, teacher, "Doctor" leader

You are NOT greater than the good shepherd, the greatest Teacher…

Jesus says, GO! Bring My lost to Me!

"Go to the highways..." (Luke 14:23)

"The poor and needy search for water, but there is none; their tongues are parched with thirst. But I the LORD will answer them; I, the God of Israel, will not forsake them."
(Is. 41:17)

"So he replied to the messengers, 'Go and report to John what you have seen and heard: The blind receive sight, the lame walk, those who have leprosy are cleansed, the deaf hear, the dead are raised, and the good news is proclaimed to the poor.'"
(Luke 7:22)

"Then he will say to those on his left, 'Depart from me, you who are cursed...For I was hungry and you gave me nothing to eat, I was thirsty and you gave me nothing to drink. I was a stranger and you didn't invite me in, I needed clothes and you did not clothe me, I was sick and in prison and you did not look after me.'" (Mat. 25:42-43)

"The spirit of the Lord is on me, because he has anointed me to proclaim the good news to the poor. He has sent me to proclaim freedom for the prisoners and recovery of sight for the blind, to set the oppressed free, to proclaim the year of the Lord's favor."
(Luke 4:18-19)

Prayer;

_____
_____
_____
_____
_____
_____
_____
_____
_____

The Hireling's Church is Killing My Sheep

To the largest organization
You say, you are several strong
Yet, you let corrupt leaders kill my sheep
You're known for hooping and hollering
Yet, gangs take over the street
You think you are strong, but you are weak
You represent Me, like I'm a weakling too
Some of the best of you
Sticking around, to make a change
Yet, you are the same. Money your aim
I did not say, stick around with an evil church
I said, to expel the evil one, doing the hurt
And if the evil one is your leader, then flee
My sheep hear, but you don't follow Me
You don't care, what you read
You don't care, what I SAY
But you will have your day
The gangs on the street
Are nothing compared to you
You're the real gangsta'
You come into My Father's house and steal
You come into My pasture and kill
I mean nothing to you
You're obsessed with your image
Your lies, and your women
Your houses and cars and living large
You are my bride, the light of the world
The salt of the earth…
The seasoning, for all My children to be rebirthed
Yet, you act, more like a whore. You know me no more
For sure you are a cult. Made up of wolves, hirelings and goats…

> *"…It is written, 'My house shall be called a house of prayer,' but you make it a den of robbers."*
>
> *(Mat. 21:13)*

"REPENT!
For the kingdom of heaven has come near."
(Mat. 3:2)

*"It isn't my responsibility to judge outsiders, but
... it certainly is your responsibility to judge those inside the
church who are sinning.
God will judge those on the outside; but as the Scriptures say,
'You must remove the evil person from among you.'"*
(1 Cor. 5:12-13)

*"They will act religious, but they will reject the power that
could make them godly. Stay away from people like that!"*
(2 Tim. 3:5)

*"But I will come -and soon- if the Lord lets me, and then I'll find
out whether these arrogant people just give pretentious speeches
or whether they really have God's power."*
(1 Cor. 4:19)

"Repent, for the kingdom of heaven is at hand."
(Mat. 3:2)

Prayer;

_____
_____
_____
_____
_____
_____
_____
_____
_____
_____
_____
_____
_____
_____
_____
_____

FIRE! Sound the Alarm

These hirelings are lying
They've been BOUGHT!
'They' no longer go to the highways
The lost, they have, FORGOT!
Scared of the gang member
How? Jesus says…
We'll pick up snakes with safety
And lay hands on the sick
If, the preacher doesn't believe
He should not be preaching
Because in fear, he is leading
A student, is like their teacher
Turning out, a bunch of weak sheep
Unhealthy and dying. Now that's deep
And the answer, 'emotional' church
Is not, just sweating, and yelling on TV
The answer is, captives being set-free
Where is the strength, of the flock?

> "The Spirit of the LORD is on me, for he has anointed me to bring good news to the poor. He has sent me to proclaim that captives will be released, that the blind will see, that the oppressed will be set free and that the time of the LORD's favor has come."
> (Luke 4:18-19)

SHEPHERDS LEAD! SHEPHERDS LEAD SHEEP!
So, who's leading the revival, to the street!
Let me answer. The shepherd is home, in his luxury
Watching his TV, picking out his suit, for Sunday
Wife at the mall, shopping. ARE YOU KIDDING ME!
Everyone will not buy into the truth, and that's okay
Cause when it's all over, Jesus STILL has the first and LAST say
"You have turned My Father's house into a den of thieves"
A den is a 'family' of thieves, not just one wolf, but many
If you truly have power, the streets and prisons, need you this hour!
If you're a real soldier in the family of Christ. You know God's word is right
You also know, what time it is. The kingdom of God is at hand! Need all warriors to
Stand! The streets must get free! Get out of your church facility, doing fake ministry!
Get to the street! Go get your Father's lost sheep! The lost are dying, going to hell…

THE PREACHERS ARE FOR HIRE!
YOUR NEIGHBOR'S HOUSE IS ON FIRE!
They have brainwashed you. Totally lied on the truth
When is the last time, a drug addict has been in your service?
And a gang member got nervous. You seriously, don't see these leaders
Workin' for that money. If they cared about Me, they'd go get little Johnny!

"Has this house, which bears my Name, become a den of robbers to you? But I have been watching! Declares the LORD." (Jere. 7:11)

"they will pick up snakes with their hands; and when they drink deadly poison, it will not hurt them at all; they will place their hands on sick people, and they will get well." (Mark 16:18)

"He said to them, 'The scriptures declare, My Temple will be a house of prayer,' but you have turned it into a den of thieves." (Luke 19:46)

"having the appearance of godliness, but denying it's power. Avoid such people." (2 Tim. 3:5)

"Then the master told the servant, 'Go out to the roads and country lanes and compel them to come in, so that my house will be full. I tell you, not one of those who were invited will get a taste of my banquet.'" (Luke 14:23-24)

"Then he said to his disciples, 'The harvest is plentiful but the workers are few. Ask the Lord of the harvest, therefore, to send out workers into his harvest field.'" (Mat. 9:37-38)

Prayer;

_____
_____
_____
_____
_____
_____
_____
_____

Something is Wrong...Very Wrong

Has the local Church has lost her power?
Think about it. Are, we blind to this hour?
We are now living, in the very last days
Sugar coating the gospel and turning away
When, you hear a leader, 'often' speaking
From, a 'covering sin' point of view
Normally, this is because, he is sinning too
He creates, that everywhere we turn, we sin
He likes to say, "Paul had a thorn in his flesh."
The bible says, "so he would not be conceited"
It does not say, so 'Paul' could keep on sinning
When a leader wants to lead, yet can't live holy
This hurts the church, making the sheep, believe
That holy living, unto our Lord, cannot be achieved
Yet, Christ requires holiness. Without which, no man shall see the Lord
I can only beg, that you would read your bible
Stop depending on preachers, for your survival
You are being led, like sheep to the slaughter
Satan is destroying, our sons and daughters
Why do you think, Satan can take over a city?
If, greater is He, that is within you and me
Because, that power comes with a, 'Jesus' lifestyle
Just read the word, you'll see it's true
Is your leader, training you, to win the lost?
Many are likely not. The few that are, are very few
Jesus says, false prophets and false teachers are many...
STUDY! Why won't they point us, to Christ and His lost sheep
Jesus Christ says, our life should be like His. For others we should live
Most 'Churches', are not going out, to share His way. Something is wrong
We better find out what it is. It may, not be for Jesus Christ, they really live
Christ says, you cannot serve God and Money. You must GO into YOUR city!

> "Be holy because I am holy."
>
> (1 Pet. 1:16)

Something is wrong, we better find out what it is
Holiness in Christ...is this truly, what your preacher lives?
You are smart, just get a pen. List the following; PRISON – HUNGRY
HOMELESS – SICK – DRUG ADDICT - ORPHANS – ALCOHOLIC
POVERTY – DISEASED - HOOD MINISTRY - MURDERERS, KILLIN'
WITH A SPIRIT OF REVENGE. WHO ARE WE DELIVERIN'?

"For it is time for judgement to begin at the household of God;
and if it begins with us, what will be the outcome for those
who do not obey the gospel of God? And if the righteous is
scarcely saved, what will become of the
ungodly and the sinner?"
(1 Peter 4:17-18)

"And these signs will accompany those who believe: in my name
they will cast out demons; they will speak in new tongues; they
will pick up serpents with their hands; and if they drink any
deadly poison, it will not hurt them; they will lay their hands
on the sick, and they will recover."
(Mark 16-18)

"The people also gathered from the towns around Jerusalem,
bringing the sick and those afflicted with unclean
spirits, and they were all healed."
(Acts 5:16)

Prayer;

_____
_____
_____
_____
_____
_____
_____
_____
_____
_____
_____
_____
_____
_____
_____
_____
_____
_____

Deep Sleep

I was in a city once. It was so sad
Small area, about two thousand
One main street light, one grocery store
Not much more. For several years
I was there, back and forth
My heart, filled with tears
I actually, loved it here
I'd walk my dog. Meet kids on the block
Many, many kids! We'd talk at the store
We'd talk on the street, or at the park
We'd pray and say bye, at dark
The main pastors are hirelings here
But those here, cannot spot that fear
Pastor, opens a facility, lives in another city
He doesn't care about the people here
It's a small place, but gangs are in place
Drugs destroying the lives of our young
After church, the main pastor is gone
Five days a week, these pastors are home

> *"You are the light of the world. -like a city on a hilltop that cannot be hidden... a lamp is placed on a stand, where it gives light to everyone in the house. In the same way, let your deeds shine out for all to see, so that everyone will praise your heavenly Father."*
> *(Mat, 5:14-16)*

How, can this city get strong. How, can the lost get found, when Jesus' love
Is not around. The young have nothing to do, when they get out of school. So
The nearby prisons are full. None of the churches here, have prison ministries
Mostly what I've seen, is the pastors competing. Competing for, 'other' church folk
Not for the lost though. My heart is broken for the city
Don't count on the hirelings, to reach the plenty
It's their own stomach, that gets fed
The people of God are falsely led
The Church, could start a 'real' Church
In their home, and deliver all the hurt
But everyone makes an excuse
The sheep, have been abused
It's like, the sheep, are now at fault
Cause they were prey, and they got caught
But Jesus says, woe to the shepherds
Who scatter my sheep…

> *"And let our people learn to devote themselves to good works, so as to help cases of urgent need, and* **not be** *unfruitful."* (Titus 3:14)

Wake up church
We're in a deep, deep sleep
Jesus holds the leaders accountable. Why shouldn't we?

"For such people are not serving our Lord Christ, but their own appetites. By smooth talk and flattery, they deceive the minds of naïve people." (Rom. 16:18)

"Depart from me, you cursed, Into the eternal fire prepared for the devil and his angels...I was...sick and in prison and you did not visit me." (Mat. 25:41-43)

"...because the LORD has anointed me to proclaim good news to the poor, He has sent me to bind up the brokenhearted, to proclaim freedom to the captives and release from darkness for the prisoners, to proclaim the year of the LORDS's favor and the day of vengeance of our God, to comfort all who morn...to bestow on them a crown of beauty instead of ashes, the oil of joy instead of morning, and a garment of praise instead of a spirit of despair. They will be called oaks of righteousness, a planting of the LORD for the display of his splendor."
(Is. 61:1-3)

Prayer;

_____
_____
_____
_____
_____
_____
_____
_____
_____
_____
_____
_____
_____

Chapter Four

ADULTERESS PASTOR

CONFRONT ME PLEASE

Adulteress Pastor

Church I'm the adulteress pastor
You know, I got an evil spirit
Why won't you come and set me free
Why, do you let me scatter, God's sheep
The least you could do, is confront me
So, I won't go to hell. The many lies I tell
I've hurt so many women, so many sheep
Yet, I continue. I'm not ashamed
I play my position, just like you play a game
I've been a whoremonger, for several years
So many families, have shed so many tears
I don't care about the kids in the church
I sleep with their mom's, I do the real dirt
You don't care what I do, you scared
To find that real power of God is rare
You let me, prostitute God's Word
You love, my smart quotes you've heard
The women love it. You can shove it
I do what I want. You don't warn me
You don't warn the sheep
Hilarious, how God's word
You don't even keep
The word says, sit me down
And separate yourself from me
But, you worryin' about that money
You leaders are just like me
Are you ever, gonna' sit me down
So, I don't live this life and lose my crown
I don't love you. You don't love me
I don't love myself…

> "Sin took advantage of those commands and deceived me; it used the commands to kill me."
>
> (Romans 7:11)

> They will act religious, but they will reject the power that could make them godly. Stay away from people like that."
>
> (2 Tim. 3:5)

I'm gonna' live this life and go to hell
Because, the truth, you also refuse to tell

"Jesus said to them, 'You, faithless people! How long must I be with you? How long must I put up with you? Bring the boy to me.' When Jesus saw that the crowd of on lookers was growing, he rebuked the evil spirit. 'Listen, you evil spirit that makes this boy unable to speak and hear,' he said. 'I command you to come out of this child and never enter him again!' Then the spirit screamed and threw the boy into another violent convulsion and left him. The boy appeared to be dead. A murmur ran through the crowd as people said, 'He's dead.' But Jesus took him by the hand and helped him to his feet. And he stood up.

Afterward, when Jesus was alone in the house with the disciples, they asked him. 'Why couldn't we cast out the evil spirit?' Jesus replied, 'This kind can come out only by prayer.'" *(Mark 9:25-29)*

And he said to them, "This kind cannot come forth by nothing, but prayer and fasting." (Mark 5:29)

"For, being ignorant of the righteousness of God, and seeking to establish their own, they did not submit to God's righteousness." (Rom. 10:3)

"...In my name they will drive out demons..." (Mark 16:17)

Prayer;

_____

_____

_____

_____

_____

_____

_____

Please Rebuke my Sin, I'm Dyin'

I'm an adulteress pastor
You can watch me, in church
Or on the internet, you'll hear me
This is what I tell my sheep
I warn them a lot
Reminding them, I'm all they got
We are in 'covenant.' I rub it in
I tell them, there's no relationship
Like a shepherd and his flock
I remind them, I'm all you've got
I tell them, "I'm the keeper of your soul
Don't talk to 'speakers' I bring in."
I spend several minutes, telling them
"Come back, on the week night."
Warning them often, "If you don't
You ain't right." My entire mission
My entire - 'being' - is to raise funds
I bleed you. I need you
I am, a curse to you
I steel from you. Not help you
I'm far, from a blessing to you
I mix scriptures, with the truth
With the sisters, I have affairs
I don't love you, I don't care
No one intervenes, to stop me
No one loves me enough!
No one puts me, to a halt
I've created all the
Ingredients, for a
Cult…

> *"For if we go on sinning deliberately after receiving the knowledge of the truth, there no longer remains a sacrifice for sins, but a fearful expectation of judgement, and a fury of fire that will consume the adversaries."*
>
> *(Heb. 10:26)*

**Where are those who love me enough
I am a wolf in sheep clothe
You trust me, though**

"...beware of false prophets, who come to you."
(Mat. 7:15)

"Keep alert at all times. And pray that you might be strong enough to escape all these things that are going to take place, and to stand before the Son of Man." (Luke 21:36)

"Be on guard! Be alert! You do not know when the time will come." (Mark 13:33)

"When the Spirit of truth comes, he will guide you into all truth, for he will not speak on his own authority, but whatever he hears he will speak, and he will declare to you the things that are to come." (John 16:13)

"But When Peter came to Antioch, I had to oppose him to his face, for what he did was very wrong." (Gal. 2:11)

"But those elders who are sinning you are to reprove before everyone, so that others may take warning."
(1 Tim. 5:20)

"Therefore rebuke them sharply, that they may be sound in the faith..." (Titus 1:13)

Prayer;

_____

_____

_____

_____

_____

_____

_____

Church, will you Stop, this Hurt?

One Sunday morning, I was preaching in the pulpit
A ruckus started at the exit, the brothers took care of it
I continued the service. Their wives, a little nervous
You, think these gangs are something
They ain't got nothing on me. That was a brother
He brought his gun, coming to see me
To 'talk' about the session, I had with his fiance
I was performing, her pre-marital session
Thought, I'd give her my personal message
She must have gone back and told him
Some of those sisters, you just can't depend on them
A couple of the brothers, put him in their car
I continued my, 'delivering service' from afar
Later, when I was told, of his accusations
I informed everyone, those were fabrications
'These women' love what they see. Obsessed with me
They know they can't have me, so they lie on me
I throw in some anger and God's word
Shake my head, then act appalled
For thirty plus years, I've been tricking all
Many scriptures, could help them with me
But they don't read, they're too lazy
I got it all, set up for me. I answer to nobody
I should be accountable, to somebody
God is a God of order, but these church folks
Just won't study. They won't read
Why, are the sisters in my office, alone meeting with me?
Satan, uses disorder and trickery, to devour with ease
I am the vessel that he uses, to attack the sheep
I've hurt and split up, thousands of families
I am an adulteress pastor…

> *"Do not admit a charge against an elder except on the evidence of two or three witnesses."*
>
> *(1 Tim. 5:19)*

Church, why won't you stop this hurt? I'm killing, God's sheep
You hide my sin. I'm a wolf and I thrive within
Your Father's house is my Den

"But everything should be done in a fitting and orderly way."
(1 Cor. 14:40)

"The reason I left you in Crete was that you might put in order what was left unfinished and appoint elders in every town, as I directed you"
(Titus 1:5)

"Likewise, teach the older women to be reverent in the way they live, not to be slanders or addicted to much wine, but to teach what is good.
They can urge the younger women to love their husbands and children,
To be self-controlled and pure, to be busy at home, to be kind, and to be subject to their husbands, so that no one maligns the Lord of God.
Similarly, encourage the young men to be self-controlled. In everything set them an example by doing what is good. In your teaching show integrity, seriousness and soundness of speech that cannot be condemned, so that those who oppose you may be ashamed because they have nothing bad to say about us."
(Titus 2:3-8)

Note: Set up order for counseling sessions. Give the older women the charge of meeting with and assisting the younger women. Let the Pastor stay focused on the larger mission of the church, to reach the lost.

Prayer;

_____
_____
_____
_____
_____
_____
_____
_____
_____

The Wages of Sin is Death

Sin is death,
Yet, you speak constantly of covering it up
We expose sin. Yet, love the one which holds it in
If, I'm sleeping with my boyfriend
Come, tell me it's wrong. Fight for me to, live
Tell me to repent, and ask the Lord to forgive
Don't cover it up, and let me die, in my sin
Love me through it
But love me the way, the Lord, says to do it
Tell me, I must turn
Tell me, Satan wants me, to burn
Tell me, God has provided, a way out
That I would forever, live free, from doubt
Tell me, Jesus is the way!
And whatever I choose, you'll love me anyway
God hates sin. Why do you, conceal it within
If your child, gets ready to stick metal, in a plug
What do you say, "Oh baby, come give me a hug?"
No! Satan is a liar! Snatch that baby, from the fire
Warn that child. Correct that child. Love that child
When 'that child' is a man. The same principle stands
Snatch him from the fire. Don't let him live, in sin's desire
If your pastor, is sleeping with the brother's wives
Open your blinded, betrayed, bewitched eyes
Stop living naïve. Stop believing in the lies
Where sin is allowed, everyone dies
Stop teaching, you are to cover it
You cover the sinner, not the sin…

"The wages of sin, is death, the gift of God is eternal life."

(Rom. 6:23)

Sin equals death, when it's held within
"For the wages of sin is death."
My friend
(Romans 6:23)

"Have nothing to do with the fruitless deeds of darkness, but rather expose them. It is shameful even to mention what the disobedient do in secret." (Eph. 5:11-12)

"Who will rise up for me against the wicked? Who will stand for me against those who practice iniquity?" (Ps. 94:16)

"Judge not according to appearance, but judge righteous judgement." (John 7:24)

"Do you not know the saints will judge the world? And if the world is to be judged by you, are you incompetent to try trivial cases?" (1 Cor. 6:2)

"The Lord said to Joshua, "Stand up, what are you doing down on your face? Israel has sinned; they have violated my covenant which I commanded them to keep. ... that is why the Israelites cannot stand against their enemies... I will not be with you anymore unless you destroy whatever among you is devoted to destruction." (Josh. 7:10-12)

Note: We have the Holy Spirit to guide us, to live holy.
"God is the same yesterday, today and forever." (Heb. 13:8)

Prayer to remove sin from the church;

_____

_____

_____

_____

_____

_____

New Creature in Christ...Right?

After I joined, I heard the secretary was seeing him
Both, married with a family, but I had my own sin
I had just moved away, from my, young husband
Who was cheating back then. I came to a new city
A new church, started over again. Got settled in
I was really happy, made some good friends
So, I thought, back then. Then a girl joined
With, her husband and family, called me
"I'm here at the church, with him, now"
I'm wondering, this concerns me, how
She says, "Well, we're not working
On a project, we've been intimate."
She's excited, she actually tells me
Which room, she's in. Tells me to
come and look, if I don't believe
I pass the information on, to family
But not much he could do, it's his boss too
I help the girl through it, tryin' to save her family
Lord help her. Help her family! Lord please, help me
Before it settles in… here comes another 'godly' friend
She was such a holy missionary to me. I so loved her family
I'd watch the 'church' television show. I hurt so. I watched
Them do, those fakes messages though, "Saving the lost souls"
Then shattered, my world. Here comes another, 'church' girl
Telling me, about phone sex. And it gets steamy in the church office
Are you kidding me! My children call you, Auntie. Another friend
And this is the shepherd, that is to pray for our soul. He's really just a
Disobedient child. Running wild. .Playin' at the church, like he's in daycare
Drooling on the baby doll toys. Church, are you gonna' correct, this self-centered
Out of control, boy?

> *"Anyone who is in Christ is a new creature, all things have past, away and behold all things have become new."*
> *(2 Cor. 5:17)*

Satan comes to steal, kill and destroy. He's a jerk, an abuser, a user
Killing God's family. Killing God's ministry
Killing God's… "me"

"And a servant who knows what the master wants, but isn't prepared and doesn't carry out those instructions, will be severely punished." (Luke 12:47)

"So whoever knows the right thing to do and fails to do it, for him it is sin." (James 4:17)

"'If you were blind, you wouldn't be guilty,' Jesus replied. 'But you remain guilty because you claim you see." (John 9:41)

"Do you see a man who is wise in his own eyes? There is more hope for a fool than for him." (Pro. 26:12)

"For the wisdom of this world is foolishness to God. As the Scriptures say, 'He traps the wise in the snare of their own cleverness.'" (1 Cor. 3:19)

"But now I am writing to you not to associate with anyone who bears the name of brother if he is guilty of sexual immorality or greed, or is an idolater, reviler, drunkard, or swindler-not even to eat with such a one." (1 Cor.5:11)

"They claim to know God, but by actions they deny him. They are detestable, disobedient and unfit for doing anything good." (Titus 1:16)

Prayer

_____

_____

_____

_____

_____

My Sister's Keeper

I, often work with the youth. They, totally got my heart
I like to play board games, sports and watch movies with them
At church, I would help the kids; and of course, enjoy myself
Well, I began to see my 'sisters' coming and going into the office
I noticed, when 'he' wasn't around, they would look, 'different'
But, when he was in his office, they would get all, dolled up
Going home after work, showering, freshening up, all made up
It became so noticeable. I could pick them out, almost blindfolded
Every hair, in place. Fresh make-up on, their face. Smiling in, his face
I, thought it would all get better. Surely, these sister's families mattered
Instead, all the families, are now gone. Some, divorced. No one strong!
And children, grew up, with resentment. Being so young, and seeing it
This, is not a history, of women being, 'unknowingly' a little too nice
And then, accidently stumbling upon an adulteress affair, at church. No!
This, is a terrible evil spirit, sent by Satan, to destroy the children of God
The bible says, guard your heart. If, you have a ministry, set up a policy
Guidelines, in place, to protect. Put up a shield. Guard, against every evil
Jesus says to shun, even the very appearance of evil. Jesus is forever wise
He knows, 'the appearance of,' can turn in, to more than meets the eyes
Start a, Sister's Keeper prayer group. Let the sisters know, you are there
Ready to pray. To help. To care. Support one another. Guard our brothers
We, are not unaware of Satan's schemes. No excuse, to allow sin, in church
Jesus has given us, specific and clear guidelines. We are sisters, in the Lord
How about, 'good lookin' out?' Don't we all, lock our doors, for safety at home
It's the same, for our church home. Safety is key. Defend and protect our family
And, do not criticize the spouse, that's being cheated on; "She or he, does this…"
Don't make excuses, for sin. When a problem does arise, get rededicated, to Christ
Some, tried to defend the pastor's actions. But, the victims, at this pastor's hand
Came, in all shapes, all colors and SIZES! A few were much larger, than his wife
You can't make excuses for sin. Just realize, with Satan, you NEVER, ever win!

Satan has one agenda; to destroy the children of God
Open your eyes. Expose and remove sin
Or your church family
Will pay the price

"Don't be misled- you cannot mock the justice of God. You will always harvest what you plant. Those who live to satisfy their sinful nature, will harvest decay and death from that sinful nature. But those who live to please the Spirit will harvest everlasting life from that Spirit. So let's not get tired of doing what is good. At just the right time we will reap a harvest of blessing if we do not give up." (Gal. 6:7-9)

"A friend is always loyal, and a brother is born to help in time of need." (Pro. 17:17)

"Two people are better off than one, for they can help each other succeed. If one person falls, the other can reach out and help. But someone who falls alone is in real trouble." (Eccl. 4:9)

"Dear brothers and sisters, if another believer is overcome by sin, you who are godly should gently and humbly help that person back onto the right path. And be careful not to fall into the same temptation yourself. Share each other's burdens, and in this way obey the law of Christ." (Gal. 6:1-2)

"...'My temple shall be called a house of prayer,' but you have turned it into a den of thieves!" (Mat. 21:13)

"The path of the virtuous leads away from evil." (Pro. 16:17)

Prayer for ungodly situations to be revealed and restored;

_____
_____
_____
_____
_____
_____

No more - I

I remember way back when I
I joined the church and made some friends
Then, my life experience, was so shaken
And unlike ever, my heart was breakin'
Incredible pain. As I watched, the insane
How, could you think, he was yours
When, you already had, yours
And he already had his
My father teaches us how to, live
Would you sacrifice, your family's life?
Greatest blessing on earth, 'my family'
I was cut deep. Gut out, to the core
Begged, for that pain, to be no more
I got, a really soft and tender heart
Tried to live my life, and sin apart
This pain, surely, damaged me
Decades later, I'm still not free
You see, it was also my family…
My church family
These were, my sisters and brothers
And you helped split us, from each other
So, you think you can come, into the church
And live like a whore. My Father says, **No more**
Exposed you will be. Can't keep breakin' up families
You dress like a missionary. And think you're a queen
But, when you sneak and sleep with the pastor, our shepherd
You're none of those things. It makes you unattractive, ugly inside
You've now become a whore. No! No! No! Can't soften it, anymore
Whores, tear up family. All participants, have torn up my family, our family
You're 'bout to be exposed. Pastor, stop sleepin' with them "h_ _ _"
Satan is the author of lies. He comes to steal, kill and destroy…

> *"I have stored up your word in my heart, that I might not sin against you."*
>
> *(Psalm 119:11)*

> *"Who can find a trustworthy man?"*
> *(Pro. 20:6)*

No More!
Stand for what is right
Pray for sisters and brothers in this fight
We've got to get strong! Sinners are losing their life

"Flee from sexual immorality. All other sins a person commits are outside the body, but whoever sins sexually, sins against their own body." (1 Cor. 6:18)

"Thou must not commit adultery." (Ex. 20:14)

"You have heard that it was said, 'You shall not commit adultery.'
But I say to you that everyone who looks at a woman with lustful Intent
has already committed adultery with her in his heart."
(Mat. 5:28)

"For the scriptures say, 'You must be holy because I am holy.'"
(1 Pet. 1:16)

"For we are not fighting against flesh-and-blood enemies, but against evil rulers and authorities of the unseen world, against mighty powers in this dark world, and against evil spirits in the heavenly places." (Eph. 6:12)

"You dear children, are from God and have overcome them, because the one who is in you is greater than the one who is in this world." (1 John 4:4)

Prayer;

_____
_____
_____
_____
_____
_____
_____
_____

No More - II

Preachers stop lyin'
God is not, 'always' smilin'
He hurts too. He loves all of us
All of you. Woe to the pastor
Scattering My sheep
Does that sound like
He's some 'punk' Daddy
You better study your word
My Father needs to be heard
You may lift your eyes in hell
If the truth, you refuse to tell
As we continue to speak, of Grace
His Grace, Amazing! I can't explain it!
How he shed His blood, on CALVARY
Gave His life, to save and make us free
He alone, is the Answer for this world!
For every man, woman, boy and girl
But you have to teach the 'entire' word
He says, 'Do not grieve the Holy Spirit'
Grief, is sorrow, pain, wounds, distress
To break someone's heart, to lament
And, you don't think, He's unhappy?
You sleepin' with His daughter's
Yeah, you 'better ask somebody'
Ask a Father, of a Daddy's girl
Often she's, his only world
She walks in, as a visitor
You thinkin' like a whore
Thinkin' what you wanna' do. She on the alter, tryna' get brand new
Soon, as she gets in your counseling session. Satan begins, his deceitful
Mission. Church sisters, and mothers, you killin' me. Why, are 'you' not helping -
With her life's ministry?

> "And do not bring
> sorrow to God's
> Holy Spirit
> by the way you live.
> Remember, he has
> identified you as his
> own, guaranteeing
> that you will be
> saved on the day
> of redemption."
>
> (Eph. 4:30)

Pastor, if you mean no harm, stop meeting with the sisters alone
You better be sure, purity in heart
Is what you have sown!

*"How often they rebelled against him in the wilderness and **grieved him** in the desert." (Ps. 78:40)*

"Many times he delivered them, but they were rebellious in their purposes and were brought low through their iniquity." (Ps. 106:43)

"To the Lord our God belong mercy and forgiveness, for we have rebelled against him." (Daniel 9:9)

"Instead, clothe yourself with the presence of the Lord Jesus Christ. And don't let yourself think about ways to indulge your evil desires." (Rom. 13:14)

"... but his delight is in the law of the Lord, and on his law he meditates day and night." (Ps. 1:2)

"Blessed are the pure in heart, for they shall see God." (Mat. 5:8)

"God is not a God of disorder..." (1 Cor. 14:33)

"Delight yourself in the Lord, and he will give you the desires of your heart." (Psalm 37:4)

Prayer;

_____
_____
_____
_____
_____
_____
_____
_____
_____
_____
_____

VICIOUS WOLVES

My pastor, sent our family away
So, I wouldn't ruin his plans, those days
Expose, what I had been told, by my friends
But actually, shocked, I was keeping it all in
Stressed and praying, it would all soon end
Thinking to myself, we would all pray
And he, would get some help
I believed, that's how it should be
That we would just pray and believe
Ending with, a tremendous testimony
Instead, I was sent away, to another city
Because, I had married into, 'the family'
I was devastated, but didn't really know it
Left my mom, now she's gone
Left my cousins, my family and good friends
Though other friends, were sleeping with him
I left, what I believed to be, a pretty good life
Because, of that lust demon, he chose to hide
We, have power, if we don't hold on to pride
He, allowed those demons to split the church
Families divorced, decades later, it still hurts
I want to ask the pastors now
That are involved in this type of lifestyle…
How much is it worth, for so many sheep to hurt
It must have been, thousands of lives affected
And all the children… that were neglected
Our pastor, sleeping with the church children's moms
While, hugging their neck…
Eating with their dads, at the 'prayer' breakfast
Talkin' 'bout, "What the heck."

> *"The hired hand runs away because he's working only for the money and doesn't really care about the sheep."*
> *(John 10:13)*

> *"For where you have envy and selfish ambition, there you find disorder and every evil practice."*
>
> *(James 3:16)*

**…Jesus has warned you, "these hirelings
Don't care about you."
(John 10:13)**

"Whoever walks in integrity walks securely, but he who makes his way crooked will be found out." (Pro. 10:9)

"Beware of false prophets who come disguised as harmless sheep but are really vicious wolves. You can identify them by their fruit, that is by the way they act... A good tree produces good fruit and a bad tree produces bad fruit. So every tree that does not produces good fruit is cut down and thrown into the fire. Yes, just as you can identify a tree by its fruit, so you can identify people by their actions." (Mat. 7:15-20)

"Whoever says he abides in him ought to walk in the same way in which he walked." (1 John 2:6)

"But I will continue doing what I have always done. This will undercut those who are looking for an opportunity to boast that their work is just like ours. These people are false apostles. They are deceitful workers who disguise themselves as apostles of Christ. But I am not surprised! Even Satan disguises himself as an angel of light. So it is no wonder that his servants also disguise themselves as servants of righteousness. In the end they will get the punishment their wicked deeds deserve." (2 Cor. 11:12-15)

Prayer, that wolves, false prophets will be exposed;

_____
_____
_____
_____
_____
_____

Do Not Associate with Evil...

Evil spirits...
Greed spirit. Lust spirit
Why can't we just, cast it out
The leader often, may not want it out
Selfish ambition, opens the door
To every evil work
Greed sets in. Lust wins
A believer, who stumbles
Will, want to be delivered
But for the Pastor, who is *not* a sheep
Jesus says, Flee. When a leader continues
In sin, tearing down the women within
Warn him
Expose him
Expel him
Flee from him
The Saints that try to, cover him
Are confused about God's word
Expelling, is done in love
It's a reprimand from above
God chastises, to save his life
And to save the life, of the sheep
To be able to graze, in a pasture of safety
How do you, leave a wolf in your mist
And not expose him?
Would, you leave a killer, in your home
Living, among your loved ones, your family alone?
Would you let a witch, dressed in a princess outfit, babysit?
Satan's killing, Our Father's children, His sheep
The church is sleep...

> *"No one who lives in him keeps on sinning. No one who continues to sin has either seen him or known him."*
> *(1 John 3:6)*

Expose him, expel him, flee from him
Warn him. This is the love
You must have for him

"Have nothing to do with the fruitless deeds of darkness, but rather expose them." (Eph. 5:11)

"Everyone who does evil hates the Light, and does not come into the Light for fear that his deeds will be exposed." (John 3:20)

"... you must not associate with anyone who claims to be a brother or sister but is sexually immoral or greedy, an idolater or slanderer, a drunkard or swindler. Do not even eat with such people." (1 Cor. 5:11)

"If you are wise and understand God's ways, prove it by living an honorable life, doing good works with the humility that comes from wisdom." (James 3:13)

"...If you have warned the righteous man that the righteous should not sin and he does not sin, he shall surely live because he took warning; and you have delivered yourself." (Ez. 3:20)

Prayer for sin to be exposed and for redemption of God's sheep;

_____
_____
_____
_____
_____
_____
_____
_____
_____
_____

Chapter Five

BEWARE OF WOLVES

MATTHEW 7:15

Wolves are Killing the Sheep - I

The Wolves are out the den
And they're killing sheep
The wolves are out the den
Destroying God's meek
Wake up church. You are asleep
A male, pastor, recently exposed
For adultery with men
God bless him
It was all on the news
His wife filed for divorce
God bless him
His heart broken
His tears flowin'
My heart wanted to hug him
He sought forgiveness
God restored him
His wife forgave him
What a beautiful story
To God be the Glory
Satan lost this soul
This family was restored
Thank you Lord!
Now, in any heartbreak
Don't forget, a wolf is vicious
So obviously some sheep, did not stay at this church
Having to deal with this hurt, could not have been easy
Well, on the following Sunday. I was watching, 'Christian' TV
A pastor in the same city. Announced on national television
"If any of his members are here today, I don't want you here
Get out! Go somewhere else. I don't want you here."

My eyes filled with tears
Shepherds leading with rudeness, intimidation and fear
Jesus, open the sheep's ears. Cause them to only, your voice, hear

"For such men are false apostles, deceitful workmen, disguising themselves as apostles of Christ."
(2 Cor. 11:13)

"'Woe to the shepherds who are destroying and scattering the sheep of my pasture!' Declares the Lord. Therefore, this is what the Lord, the God of Israel says to the shepherds who tend my people: 'Because you have scattered my flock and driven them away and have not bestowed care on them, I will bestow punishment on you for the evil you have done,' declares the Lord."
(Jere. 23:2)

"Watch out for those dogs, those evildoers, those mutilators of the flesh."
(Phil. 3:2)

Prayer;

_____
_____
_____
_____
_____
_____
_____
_____
_____
_____
_____
_____
_____
_____
_____
_____

Wolves are Killing the Sheep - II

It makes me cry
Just to think about it
So, who is to restore hurt souls
We are a family
In danger, you're not alone
You can come to my home
We work together
We don't kill each other
If sheep leave their flock
There is a reason for it
It doesn't mean, they're being mean
It doesn't mean, they want to destroy
In a crisis, they too, must be restored
Not thrown away and isolated more
What is wrong with you, shepherd!
What wisdom, did you display
In treating God's sheep this way?
Are, these sheep now responsible
For their shepherd's hidden sins?
Homosexuality with several victims
The sheep of this flock have sons
What chances, were they to take
Now believing, their shepherd is fake
The sheep in tears, the community in fear
And a neighboring shepherd's wisdom, says, "Get out, I don't want you here."
What if in fact, after service, they left. Deciding, not to come back to church
Ever …

> *"But woe to you, scribes and Pharisees, hypocrites! For you shut the kingdom of heaven in people's faces. For you neither enter yourselves nor allow those who would enter to go in."*
>
> *(Mat. 23:10)*

The wolves are out of the den. And their killing God's sheep
The wolves are out of the den. Destroying God's meek
Wake up church. You are asleep

"Many shepherds have destroyed my vineyard; they have trampled down my portion; they have made my pleasant portion a desolate wilderness." (Jere. 12:10)

"When he saw the crowds, he had compassion for them, *because they were confused and helpless, like sheep without a shepherd." (Mat. 9:36)*

"My people have been lost sheep. Their shepherds have led them astray and turned them loose in the mountains. They have lost their way and can't remember how to get back to the sheepfold." (Jere. 50:6)

Prayer;

_____
_____
_____
_____
_____
_____
_____
_____
_____
_____
_____
_____
_____
_____
_____
_____
_____

Beware of Wolves

When this truth is taught
People ask, what's this all about
It's what Jesus taught about
Beware of wolves in sheep clothes
Are we leaving, this truth alone?
What is it, we have to hide?
Isn't the Holy Spirit our guide?
Isn't this, God's written word?
Don't we obey? Haven't we heard?
How, do we silence, an alarm
When a fire's burning strong?
"It's not wise, to go to sleep
With your neighbor's house on fire"
That's a proverb from kings
Church you better wake up
The neighborhood is burning
You are comfortable in your sleep
But, to these wolves, you are meat
This is not a Robin hood story
Taking from the strong
And giving to the weak
This is Little Red Riding hood
The wolves are loose
And they're killing God's sheep!
God's houses are a den of thieves
You better, warn somebody…

> *"The scriptures declare,*
> *'My temple will be called*
> *a house of prayer,' but*
> *you have turned it into a*
> *den of thieves!"*
>
> *(Mat. 21:13)*

Jesus says;
Feed the hungry. Give drink to the thirsty. Take a stranger in
Care for the sick. Visit the prisoners. Go to the street
And compel men, to come in

"Watch out for false prophets. They come to you in sheep's clothing, but inwardly they are ferocious wolves."
(Mat. 7:15)

"Then he will say to those on his left, 'Depart from me, you who are cursed, into eternal fire prepared for the devil and his angels. For I was hungry and you gave me nothing to eat, I was thirsty and you gave me nothing to drink, I was a stranger and you did not invite me in, I needed clothes and you did not clothe me, I was sick and in prison and you did not look after me.'"
(Mat. 25:41-43)

Prayer

_____
_____
_____
_____
_____
_____
_____
_____
_____
_____
_____
_____
_____
_____
_____
_____
_____
_____

Lost Sheep

The Jesus I know
Could never plant a church
Among the hurt, and not go
The Jesus I know, could not open a facility
And keep the doors locked, all week
The Jesus I know
Could never, not reach
How, can we do so much less, than the Lord
When He said, of His great works, we would do more
We're not involved, in massive out reaching
We're missing His heart, the heart of His teaching
We've created an environment for wolves to be fed
Not an environment for sheep to be led
The wolves are feeding, off the sheep
The pasture's no longer green
The sheep are poisoned and dying
Send down your fire, Lord!
Burn up Satan's work, Lord!
Expose the hirelings, Lord
Dry up this enemy's work, Lord
That your greater works, would be more
Jesus, your children hear your heart
It's tearing us apart
Weeping in your heart
Wake up, ALL your children, Lord
Expose the wolves and hirelings, Lord
Send out your sheep, as laborers, Lord. The harvest is plenty the laborers are few
Jesus give the young and old a vision of, YOU! Let them stop following pastors
Not following You. Sheep, Jesus has not hidden himself from you. You are lost
Because of the Pastor's you choose...

> "Peace be with you! As the Father has sent me, I am sending you."
>
> (John 20:21)

Satan knows God's word. This is how he dresses as sheep
You know God's voice, and God says, flee
Why are you not, doing greater works, than He?

"Very truly I tell you, whoever believes in me will do the works I have been doing, and they will do even greater things than these, because I am going to the Father." (John 14:12)

"These were his instructions to them: "The harvest is great, but the workers are few. So pray to the Lord who is in charge of the harvest; ask him to send more workers into his fields."
(Luke 10:2)

"Don't you have a saying, 'It's still four months until harvest'? I tell you, open your eyes and look at the fields!
They are ripe for harvest." (John 4:35)

"Look how far you have fallen! Turn back to me and do the works you did at first. If you don't repent, I will come and remove your lampstand from its place among the churches."
(Rev. 2:5)

"Wake up! Strengthen what remains and is about to die, for I have found your deeds unfinished in the sight of my God. Remember, therefore, what you have received and heard; hold it fast, and repent. But if you do not wake up, I will come like a thief, and you will not know at what time I will come to you."
(Rev. 3:3)

Prayer;

_____
_____
_____
_____
_____
_____
_____
_____
_____
_____

Beware of Destructive Heresies

I was concerned about some preaching, I heard
So, I looked up, this well- known pastor, on line
Then, I begin my chores, listening to his message
He was considered, an anointed man, highly educated
Surely, he was not wrong. But, still when I hear something
That doesn't register, that doesn't sound like my Father's voice
I have to look it up. Plus, the message was sounding really deep
Many! Many, were listening, taking notes and speaking about him
I couldn't put my finger on it, so I just kept listening, waiting
He, was on point, but something wasn't right, I pondered
I began to think. I hadn't yet heard, a particular word
I hadn't heard, the name, of God's Son. All of a sudden, I hit replay
Stared, at my lap top screen and thought, surely he didn't say that
I pushed play, again and heard him say, "Nobody wants to hear
About, no blood and nails. Tell them about the kingdom."
I played it again and again and again. And Oh, how I cried
How it hurt me inside! How he referred to my Savior, my Lord, my Christ
We, God's children, can get so caught up, wanting to be, deep and mysterious
But how, Christ saved me, when He shed His blood for me, ON CALVARY!!
If you don't want to talk about it, please, allow me! THE ONLY WAY…
To the Father, is through the Son, HIS SON! The one that died, on Calvary!
His blood washed away my sins! Gave me an incredible new life within!
I'm sold out to Him! I got no doubt in Him! He's my best friend!
He talks with me. He walks with me. I'm not confused. False prophets are
They want to tell you, all about the kingdom and leave out, "The King"
This is why they are NOT consumed, with His anointing
Because of their 'preaching', captives are **not** being set free
God says, this is my beloved Son, in whom I am well pleased. He sets captives free
We have forgotten, why sickness and disease leave, because of Jesus Christ…
On Calvary!

He rose with all power over death and life. He is the way, the truth and the life!
Every Kingdom has a king. So, when you preach His kingdom…
REMEMBER THE KING!

"Then Jesus came to them and said, 'All authority in heaven and on earth has been given to me.'" (Mat. 28:18)

*"But false prophets also arose among the people, just as there will be false teachers among you, who will secretly bring in destructive heresies, even denying the Master who bought them, **bringing upon themselves swift destruction.** And many (numerous, countless, crowds a multitude) will follow their sensuality, and because of them the way of truth will be blasphemed,"*
(2 Pet. 2:1)

"And I will do whatever you ask in My name, so that the Father may be glorified in the Son." (John 14:13)

*"When the seventy-two disciples returned, they joyfully reported to him, 'Lord, even the demons obey us when we **use your name!" (Luke 10:17)***

"Jesus said to him, 'I am the way, and the truth, and the life. No one comes to the Father except through Me.'"
(John 14:6)

Prayer

_____
_____
_____
_____
_____
_____
_____

Satan Snatches the Word

Wolves will say, this message, you're reading isn't real
Because their intent, is to destroy and steal
Snatching the word, as soon as it's heard
It's their specialty
But Jesus Christ is greater than he
Jesus says, hold on to Me
Remember, I'm your Father
My job is to protect you
My child, I have warned you
Beware of wolves in sheep clothing
Beware of leaders that are hirelings
They are more focused on their pay
This is My word, this is their way
It needs to be heard, at this time
The children being lost, are Mine
I need a revival, stop settling on survival
Snatch My children from the hands of the enemy
Stop serving in churches, not built for Me
I said, you will follow My voice
And from another, you will flee
Wake up from your slumber and follow Me!
Many books say, stay in your church
That's not the word from Me
My sheep hear My voice
Another, they will not follow, they will …FLEE!
It's a hard word, My child. It's like raising your own child
They're focused on just one thing, while you're trying to give wisdom, on everything
Get under a pastor, a leader, who is following Me! And My mission will explode
How will you know? Because I Am power. Like nothing you've ever seen
I'm healing, delivering and holy power and I'm integrity
I, Am in the prison, in the sick home, I Am unclothed
And I'm all alone, I'm a stranger and I'm hungry…

> "Like greedy dogs, they are never satisfied. They are ignorant shepherds, all following their own path and intent on personal gain"
>
> (Is. 56:11)

Your leaders, have forgotten Me
Wake up My sheep! Open your blinded eyes and see
Where is My powerful work among the hurt, in the community

*"I have no one else like Timothy, who genuinely cares about your welfare. All the others care only for themselves and not for **what matters to Jesus Christ.**" (Phil. 2:20-21)*

"They profess to know God, but they deny him by their works. They are detestable and disobedient, worthless for doing anything good."(Titus 1:16)

"They are pure in their own eyes, but they are filthy and unwashed." (Pro.30:12)

*"Having the appearance of godliness, but denying its power. **Avoid such people.**" (2 Tim. 3:5)*

> *"My sheep listen to my voice; I know them, and they follow me."*
> *(John 10:27)*

...Follow Me

- Jesus

Prayer for evil to be exposed;

_____
_____
_____
_____
_____
_____
_____
_____
_____
_____
_____
_____

Wolves Seek to Destroy Your Family

A wolf will destroy your family
During the course of this writing
I encountered many, with 'wolf' stories
One, sister says, "My husband and I almost
Divorced. We, had to move to a different city
My husband, was our pastor's armor bearer
And when our pastor's affairs, were discovered
It hurt my husband so bad, he could hardly recover
And though, it's been many years, my husband feels
Responsible because he didn't protect, all the sisters
He doesn't understand, why he never saw it."
She further states, "He beats himself up
And it's hard for either of us, to trust"
This is why it's called, spiritual warfare
It's a war on your mind, a war on your heart
Meant to hurt, destroy and tear you apart
The wolf and the hireling, don't care for you
Satan, has put them in place, to kill and destroy you
People may say, "Oh, get over it." This is true. But sheep, are overcome with guilt
From not being able to protect and then often unfortunately, deeply filled with regret
We, as a church, are not obedient in selecting pastors. That decision, damages us!
Jesus says, if a Pastor cannot rule, his own house, he cannot, come in and rule mine
We must start observing and discerning. My pastor of long ago, was having so many
Affairs, he now has, what appears to be a reprobate mind. He is still pastoring, lost
His anointing. He was cheating on his wife, for twenty years. After divorcing, he still
Sees some, from his affairs. Back then, we were led, by his excusing, his abusive sin
His wife finally found out, about him. One 'sister' has waited twenty years. I was
New at 'this' life, when she expressed to me, during the time he was married
"I'm gonna' wait for him to leave his wife." She could not have known cause'
Neither did I, how my heart emptied inside. Her condition of soul, did not
Even know, not to tell me this. Those she spoke of, were very close to me
My church family. He's been divorced several years. He has not married
Even if he does…

> "But the Lord stood with me and strengthened me… and he rescued me from certain death.
>
> (2 Tim. 4:17)

A Wolf comes to Kill, Steal and Destroy

"The thief comes only to steal, kill and destroy. I came that they may have life and have it abundantly."
(John 10:10)

"Be sober-minded; be watchful. Your adversary the devil, prowls around like a roaring lion, seeking someone to devour. Resist him, firm in your faith, knowing that the same kinds of suffering are being experienced by your brotherhood throughout the world." (1 Pet. 5:8-9)

"Therefore, whenever we have the opportunity, we should do good to everyone —especially to those in the family of faith." (Gal. 6:10)

"for if someone does not know how to manage his own household, how can he care for the church of God? (1 Tim. 3:5)

"Do not despise prophecies, but test everything; hold fast to what is good. **Abstain from every form of evil.** Now may the God of peace make you holy in every way, and may your whole spirit, soul and body be kept blameless until our Lord Jesus Christ comes again." (1 Thess. 5 20-23)

Prayer

_____
_____
_____
_____
_____
_____
_____
_____

Wolves Seek to Destroy God's Plans, For You

Satan uses wolves to destroy God's plan
Wolves kill sheep
They steal and destroy your ministry
The soloist, may use his or her gift
This helps the wolf build his church
You will not see abundance
In ministry, to the hurt
The nearby neighbors, with sons in jail
Their sons and families, will be left for hell
A wolf does not care, about lost souls
He will push ministries that are for show
Whatever makes him or her look good
Real ministry, that labors for lost souls
He will not go!
He will ensure, the website looks holy
Listing several outreaches that are *not* active
Ministry, that never prospered
Remember, he is a wolf
He cannot bare real fruit
He is obsessed with his image
He wants to say, he has a church building
A wolf prides himself, for having an actual facility
He will ensure, he is well taken care of. His focus, will be on a second facility
Before he ever goes out into the community. He is hunting 'church' members, not
Lost souls. The community is filled with lost souls, and at no point will he begin
                    ...a plan, and go
To visit prisoners, take in the homeless, go to the elderly homes or bring in the lost
He doesn't want lost souls. They are already lost. He wants church members, to lose
Their lives. Lots of church members are easy prey
They follow counterfeit, easy…

Real Sheep follow Jesus

"Whoever says, He abides in him ought to walk in the same way in which he walked." (1 John 2:6)

"For such men are false apostles, deceitful workmen, disguising themselves as apostles of Christ. And no wonder, for even Satan disguises himself as an angel of light. So it is no surprise if his servants, also, disguise themselves as servants of righteousness. Their end will correspond to their deeds." (2. Cor. 11:13-15)

"Satan comes to steal, kill and destroy..." (John 10:10)

"...For we are not unaware of his schemes."
(2 Cor. 2:11)

Prayer;

_____
_____
_____
_____
_____
_____
_____
_____
_____
_____
_____
_____
_____
_____
_____
_____
_____
_____
_____

Wolf Protégé

The following, I witnessed
A wolf teaching his protégé…
"When speaking to others, keep it moving
Say what they want to hear, for the moment
When they are explaining what they need
Say, "Call me, just call me." Keep movin'
Man, if they don't want me as their pastor
They won't have nothing. I built that church
Sell that property, get my money, get out of there."
Then, when none of the deacons, would sign to sell
The protégé pastor, forged all church officer's names
Took paper work, for all property to the bank closing
And left town, closing the plan, to leave the Church
With nothing. And nothing, was what they each had
By the time info was disclosed, protégé' was gone
And Church members in tears and heartbroken
A wolf cares nothing about God's real sheep
During separating, the wife asked her protégé, husband
What about the kids? Can you stay in town for the kids?
The wolf teacher said, "No, he doesn't need to stay.
Church people, all in your business. He needs to get out of town. He doesn't need
To be around." The children involved, never matter to wolves! Only in appearance
Do children matter. Remember, it's not what they say, it's what they do. A wolf's
Nature is savage. He cannot hide his nature. He is a killer. His fulltime mission, is to
Destroy the prey. The elderly mothers at the church, cried and cried. With a broken
Heart, soon they died. Church home lost, at the fragile and elderly cost
When wolves get to fighting, all are fair game. The children and
Elderly alike, are torn apart. A wolf prides himself
On tearing down the weak. When the wolf
Was confronted, about these affairs
He screams, "All here are jealous
But, God will fight my battles
Touch not, my holy mantle…

"…I know your deeds; you have a reputation of being alive, but you are dead."

(Rev. 3:1)

Jesus my Lord, wolves are being exposed…
Their church, will Not grow
This is your word, Lord

"Have nothing to do with the fruitless deeds of darkness, **but rather expose them. It is shameful to mention** *what the disobedient do in secret. But everything exposed by the light becomes visible- and everything that is illuminated becomes a light." (Eph. 5:12-13)*

"The hired hand is not the shepherd and does not own the sheep. So when he sees the wolf coming, he abandons the sheep and runs away. Then the wolf attacks the flock and scatters it." (John 10:12)

"...when people keep on sinning, it shows that they belong to the devil, who has been sinning since the beginning. But the Son of God came to **destroy the works of the devil."** *(1 John 3:8)*

"Beware of false prophets..." *(Mat. 7:15)*

Prayer;

_____

_____

_____

_____

_____

_____

_____

_____

_____

_____

_____

_____

Wolf Teaching

Satan's full time job, is to deceive
To turn your heart and make you believe
Believe the false, and keep you lost
He tells you, half truths. To keep you fooled
I see right through. I check the word
The greatest story ever heard
So, Imma' keep it real. He comes to steal
He's always teachin', some new revelation
Anything to keep you, from the real situation
Jesus says, to preach the kingdom. Tthis is true
Now watch how Satan, tries to trick you
Listen good! He never mentions the King
Everybody knows, every kingdom has a king
And that's how Satan gets into everything
A little bit of this and a little bit of that
Throws it all together and keeps you off track
He gets real deep, with the mysteries
Teaching all about, the Kingdom of God
It's just one problem, that I got
Jesus is the one, that came to set us, free
If he ain't home, that kingdom ain't nothin' to me
If you go to my home and I ain't there
You might encounter Scoop, layin' by the chair
If that's the case, trust me, you ain't gettin' nowhere
When I learn about God's house, Jesus needs to be home
I can't live there, on my own. But, that's what Satan's job is
To keep you off track. If, Jesus ain't talked about, you better get back
When the preachin' starts gettin' all mysterious
You better know, somethin' gettin' serious
For, all of us… Jesus was born, in a manger
Don't let anyone come, and make Him a stranger
When the preachin' starts getting' too complicated
You better watch out. Satan's job, is to fill you with doubt

If, Jesus Name, is not lifted high

I got one word for you, and that's…Bye!

"...and the sheep follow him: for they know his voice. And a stranger they will not follow, but will... flee..."
(John 10:4)

"All the prophets testify about him that everyone who believes in him receives forgiveness of sins through his name."
(Acts 10:43)

Prayer;

_____
_____
_____
_____
_____
_____
_____
_____
_____
_____
_____
_____
_____
_____
_____
_____
_____
_____

Chapter Six

PASTOR TAKE ME TO THE STREET

- LUKE 14:23

WHY WON'T YOU GO DELIVER THE GANGS?
ARE YOU WEAK? WHY WON'T YOU MENTOR
ALL THE CHILDREN, BEFORE THEY CHOOSE
THE STREET? WHO ARE YOU, REALLY?

Why won't you Go?

Pastor, why won't you go
Why won't you lead, by showing
Show us how, to win the lost
As your slogan says, at all cost
Take us to the street!
Where the sinners meet
Will, you just go, to pray
And take Jesus there, today?
Won't you lay hands on the sick
Cast out demons, with sinners, sit?
Take a street, in the neighborhood
Share, Jesus Christ and all His good
Speak life, over the families there
Lead them in, the sinner's prayer?
So many, have lost sons out there!
If you don't go, how will the lost know?
Sheep follow shepherds. Won't you go?
Do you know, it's your main job, to sow?
Sow, seeds of mercy and watch it grow
Go! Go and win the lost, with God's love
Teach the sheep how, to show God's love
Are sheep equipped, for works of service?
If, our main job, we cannot do, what then?
It's like working in a bakery, yet, never making a cake
Like, spending our life fishing, but never going to the lake
Yes, we're going to church and living, fake. Why won't you take us
To pray at the sinner's home? Why don't we go, give them a hug and just say, hi?
Thanking the Lord, that their family is alive. Why can't, we mentor their kids?
Why do we claim Christ, yet for Him we do not live?... **Why?**

**I have come to Seek and to Save
those who are lost
- Jesus**

"Then Paul and Barnabas answered them boldly: 'We had to speak the word of God to you first. Since you reject it and do not consider yourselves worthy of eternal life, we now turn to the Gentiles.'" (Acts 13:46)

*"For this is what the Lord commanded us: 'I have made you **a light for the Gentiles, that you may bring salvation** to the ends of the earth.'" (Acts 13:47)*

"... Zacchaeus stood up and said to the Lord, 'Look, Lord! Here and now I give half my possessions to the poor, and if I have cheated anybody out of anything, I will pay back four times the amount.' Jesus said to him, 'Today salvation has come to this house, because this man, too, is a son of Abraham. For the Son of Man came to seek and to save the lost.'" (Luke 19:8-10)

*"Therefore I want you to know that God's salvation has been sent to the Gentiles, **and they will listen!**" (Acts 28:28)*

"Go to the highways and hedges and compel people to come in..."
(Luke 14:23)

"...To Equip the saints for works of ministry, for building up the body of Christ..." (Eph. 4:12)

Prayer;

_____

_____

_____

_____

_____

_____

_____

If My People Would Turn

Won't you take me, to the prison?
Are you exempt, from this?
Jesus says, Depart from Me
You, did not come to see Me
If, this is not important
Why, does Jesus say it?
Upon leaving this life, physically
The last thing Jesus says, is …Go
Upon, *our* leaving this life, He says
You, did not go, or you did, go
So, how do we, stay in
Yet, this is such a priority to Him?
Our life, has turned to, taking care of me and you
'Our' family, 'our' children, 'our' sisters, 'our' brothers
What about the neighbor? The ones Jesus spoke of, the 'others'
We are dying. Losing our, 'trying'. No longer trying to win the lost
Where, is your map for this? Where, is your written vision, for this?
Where, is your heart's desire, for this? Will you continue, like this?
Have you, yet forgotten this? He that wins souls is wise
Will you, see with My eyes? He that feeds the hungry, feeds Me
He that visits the prisoner and he that visits the sick, visits Me
This, is all apart, of turning the church, from a wicked heart
"If My people, which are called by My name, will turn from
Their wicked ways..." Why won't we go to the prisons
To visit, the many hurting and lost souls? Why won't we go
To the highways and byways? Jesus says, this is My way
"Truly I tell you, the tax collectors and the prostitutes
Are entering the kingdom of God ahead of you" (Mat. 21:31)

> *"The fruit of the righteous is a tree of life, And whoever captures souls is wise."*
> *(Pro. 11:30)*

If you do not follow My ways, you are not on My highway
My way, is the highway!

*"Enter through the narrow gate. For wide is the gate and broad is the road that leads to destruction, and many enter through it. But small is the gate and narrow the road that leads to life, **and only a few find it.**" (Mat. 7:13-14)*

"The highway of the upright turns aside from evil, whoever guards his way preserves his life." (Pro. 16:17)

"The second is equally important: 'Love your neighbor as yourself.' No other commandment is greater than these." (Mark 12:31)

"...Go into the highways and hedges and compel people to come in, that my house may be filled." (Luke 14:23)

"...All authority in heaven and on earth has been given to me. Therefore go and make disciples of all nations, baptizing them in the name of the Father and of the Son and of the Holy Spirit." (Mat. 28:19)

*"For I was hungry and you didn't feed me. I was thirsty and you didn't give me a drink. I was a stranger and you didn't invite me into your home. I was naked and you didn't give me clothing. I was sick **and in prison** and you did not visit me." (Mat. 25:42-43)*

Prayer;

_____
_____
_____
_____
_____
_____
_____

WANTED:

Laborers Needed, In the Prisons, Elderly Homes & Streets

If, I went to the street
I would learn, to NOT
Take care of, just 'me'
The cares of this world
Choke, the life out of me
So, why are we obsessed
Seeking, our own success
Where are, our gifts
Needed for others?
When, will our gifts
Help, all of our brothers?
When, will we reach
With this greater love, we teach?
When will we go, to the street
And go, lay hands on the sick
That they, may be made well?
Go to the prisons. Take My word and tell
Tell of my goodness. Tell of My greatness
Tell, of My unfailing love. Tell, how I uplift. Tell, how I use gifts
Tell them all, how I change lives, and sent My Son a living sacrifice
Please, don't keep Me, to yourself. Have you totally forgotten My help?
Even you, can do nothing without Me. You were once captive, and I set you free
If, your breath left you, I can give it back. Only I deliver, from the enemy's attack
Do you remember, Me entering your life? Changing, rearranging and exchanging
Your life? I gave you beauty, when Satan planned destruction
I gave you Me, and the wisest instructions…

> "For, 'In just a little while, he who is coming will come and will not delay.'"
> (Heb. 10:37)

I have no favoritism. But, what I do have, is a shortage of laborers,
In my neighborhoods…
I want to know, will you go and compel others to come…

I, am the Father, 'you say' you serve…
I need laborers, in My kingdom!

"And will not God give justice to his elect, who cry to him day and night? Will he delay long over them? I tell you, he will give justice to them speedily. Nevertheless, when the Son of Man comes, will he find faith on earth?" (Luke 18:7-8)

"The harvest is plentiful the laborers are few..." (Luke 10:2)

"To the weak I became weak, to win the weak. I have become all things to all people so that by all possible means I might save some." (1 Cor. 9:22)

"Do nothing out of selfish ambition or vain conceit. Rather, in humility value others above yourselves, not looking to your own interests but each of you to the interests of others." (Phil. 2:4)

"But if you show favoritism, you sin..." (James 2:0)

"Still others, like seed sown among thorns, hear the word; but the worries of this life, the deceitfulness of wealth and the desires for other things come in and choke the word, making it unfruitful." (Mark 4:19)

"Until I come, devote yourself to the public reading of scripture, *to exhortation, to teaching. Do not neglect the gift you have, which was given you by prophesy when the council of elders laid their hands on you." (1 Tim. 4:13-14)*

Prayer;

_____
_____
_____
_____
_____

Fulfill Our Ministry

To fulfill our ministry, in Christ
We must work, as an Evangelist
Each of us, has this gift
Jesus says, go and do as He did
He, lived the life, of an evangelist
Jesus, did not only teach
In temples and synagogues
Jesus, went to the streets
He sat with sinners
Healed the sick
Cast out evil spirits
Fed the hungry
Clothe the naked
He, visited the prisoners
The kingdom of God, is first
The kingdom, is not talk…
But power
Stirring up our gifts
To use in God's power
Our mission is to Go!
Are we saving souls?
Setting captives free?
Reaching our community?
Pastor, can you organize
Outreach to the poor
And to the imprisoned
So, we can learn to win the lost?
Are sinners, getting saved? Getting baptized and learning Jesus' ways?
Becoming Jesus' Disciple? Then, going to reach out and continuing the cycle?
Are we making disciples, like ourselves or like Jesus? Are we going to the lost?

"…to all who did receive him, who believed in his name, he gave the right to become children of God."

(John 1:12)

"…do the work of an evangelist and fulfill your ministry…" (2 Tim. 4:5)

"For the kingdom of God is not a matter of talk, but power..."
(1 Cor. 4:20)

"Therefore, preparing your minds for action, and being sober-minded, set your hope fully on the grace that will be brought to you at the revelation of Jesus Christ." (1 Pet. 1:13)

"Stay dressed for action and keep your lamps burning."
(Luke 12:35)

"For the creation waits with eager longing for the revealing of the sons of God." (Rom. 8:19)

"He has sent me...to proclaim liberty to captives and freedom to prisoners." (Is. 61:1)

"Woe to you, teachers...Pharisees, you hypocrites! You travel over land and sea to win a single convert, and when you have succeeded, you make them twice as much a child of hell as you are." (Mat. 23:15)

Prayer for Laborers;

_____
_____
_____
_____
_____
_____
_____
_____
_____
_____
_____

Jesus, Make us Fishers of Men

If, you would just do things, His way
Souls would get saved, everyday
Acts 2:47 - God added to the church
Every day, reaching the lost and hurt
It can happen also, in the local church
It did happen. Your church is next!
Just, set up the plan. Write it plain!
Different groups of Saints, going out
To the prison, to the neighborhood
Coming back, with reports of good
Souls saved, lost, finding their way
A shepherd, physically leads sheep
To the lost, the hurt, the weak
Read and study, set up the plan
Write the vision and make it stand
Clear guidelines, with clear days and time
Clearly written, that those that read, will run
Run with understanding, of what God has done
This will build God's church…
The one you shepherd and the one worldwide
You, will be responsible for sowing, planting
And God will give the increase
He, has already spoken it, to be
It's in the atmosphere, already
Waiting for us, to walk in His promise
He has promised, to make us fishers of men. When do we begin?
As we step out, to reach the lost and the weak. He will give the increase
Souls will be saved. Adding to the kingdom, everyday…
Can only be done
His way…

> *Come follow Me…and I will make you fishers of men."*
>
> *(Mat. 4:19)*

Jesus, make us 'true' fishers of men, again!

"...they shared with anyone who was in need. With one accord they continued to meet in the temple courts and to break bread from house to house, sharing their meals with gladness **...praising God...And the Lord added to their number daily** *those who were being saved." (Acts 2:47)*

"Then the Lord said to me, Write my answer plainly on tablets, so the runner can carry the correct message to others. The vision is for a future time...it will be fulfilled. If it seems slow in coming, wait patiently, for it will surely take place. It will not be delayed." (Hab. 2:2-3)

"I planted the seed in your hearts, and Appollos watered, but God made it grow. It's not important who does the planting, or who does the watering. What's important is that God makes the seed grow." (1 Cor. 3:7)

Prayer;

_____
_____
_____
_____
_____
_____
_____
_____
_____
_____
_____
_____
_____

I AM THAT I AM

Please, Remember Me
I am Jesus
I Am the way, the truth and the life
I am your perfect friend. A very present help
Once, walked as a man. I AM that I AM
I am a Father, that wants to come in
I want to sit with you, sup with you
Live in you, speak to you, speak through you
I'm the best thing, for you
I'm not hidden, from you
I want to share My thoughts with you
Expose My plans to you. I love you
I love sharing My plans with you
I can make you laugh. Laugh until you cry
I can show you, the funniest things
When you sit and sup with Me
You could be kinda' sad, thinking
Your life, didn't go as you planned
Then, I'd have you look down, at this
Unusual creature, on the ground
It would be so unique, you'd say, Lord
What, in the world is this, and I'd say
You are special to Me this way, each day
When I look at you, I see only amazing beauty and strength
Man looks at the outside, I look at the heart. I give beauty for ashes. I know
Life's been hard. Each and every second, you're My shining star. I just need
To get your Attention, on My lost. So My children will spend eternity with Me
Bring My lost to mM. Sow seeds and believe. You must remember, you were once
Like them. You cannot leave them, in their sin…

Water seeds and leave the rest to Me. I will give the increase
Will you, get your eyes off other things
And serve Me

"God said to Moses, I AM WHO I AM. This is what you are to say to the Israelites: I AM has sent me to you.'" (Ex. 3:14)

"This command I am giving you today is not too difficult for you to understand, and it is not beyond your reach."
(Deut. 30:11)

"...God is our refuge and strength, an ever-present help in trouble." (Ps. 46:1)

"...He will give a crown of beauty for ashes, a joyous blessing instead of mourning, festive praise instead of despair. In their righteousness, they will be like great oaks that the Lord has planted for His own glory." (Is. 61:3)

"I planted the seeds in your hearts, and Apollos watered it, but it was God who made it grow." (1 Cor. 3:6)

"I will search for my lost ones who strayed away, I will bring them safely home again. I will bandage the injured and strengthen the weak. But I will destroy those who are fat and powerful. I will feed them, yes- feed them justice!" (Ez. 34:16)

"...the harvest is great, but the workers are few..." (Luke 10:2)

Prayer;

_____

_____

_____

_____

_____

_____

"I Came to Save the World"

We, help Satan destroy the world
By weakening God's word
"All things are possible with God."
To men, women, boys and girls
You, can't add your own philosophy
Even when, you personally believe
It's your greatest idea, for me
You have got to hear, from Jesus
And ask Him, what He needs
Yes, I want to go to school
Along with that, Jesus must rule
Yes, I really know, I need a job
But, don't skip over, telling me
That I'm a **REAL**, child of God
Handle me with love, delicately
Cause my life, is special to Thee
Handle me like a dove
With wise and tender love
Don't give me direction
Without His instruction and
revelation

> *"If anyone hears my words but does not keep them, I do not judge him; for I did not come to judge the world but to save the world. The one who rejects me and does not receive my words has a judge; the word that I have spoken will judge him on the last day. I have not spoken on my own authority, but the Father who sent me has himself given me…what to say and what to speak."*
> *(John 12:47-49)*

My Father, may need me, to go out into the street
Lay hands on the sinners. And set the captive free
These are the last days. The answers are in the Holy bible
Fast and pray, and live past survival. Get knowledge, sharpen your gifts
And remember, His holiness, is no myth. Lay hands on the lost and the sick
Casting out sickness and evil spirits. Raise the dead. I must do all God says
Teach the children, about the *real* anointing of Jesus Christ, what it looks like
Before they enter this enemy's fight, because Satan is playin' all his cards right
Education and a job, a MUST. But, don't fake. Jesus Christ, is your first TRUST
Seek ye first the kingdom of God and His righteousness. Fasting with prayer
Casting my cares. My Father is Almighty, and He is EVERYWHERE!
Faith without works is dead, you know. Stop handling God fake, and…
"Go!" He came to Save the World…

Go… into the highways and byways and compel
Others to come…into My Kingdom

"...I have made you a light for the Gentiles, that you may bring salvation to the ends of the earth." (Acts 13:47)

"And nations shall come to your light, and kings to the brightness of your rising." (Is. 60:3)

"...seek his kingdom, and these things will be added to you. Do not be afraid, little flock, for your Father has been pleased to give you the kingdom." (Luke 12:31-32)

"Turn to me and be saved, all you ends of the earth; for I am your God, and there is no other." (Is. 45:22)

"And the word became flesh and dwelt among us..." (John 1:14)

"Go...make disciples of all nations, baptizing them in the name of the Father and of the Son and the Holy Spirit." (Mat. 28:19)

"Is there any sick among you? let him call for the elders of the church...and the prayer of faith and he shall save the sick...." (James 5:15)

"Trust in the Lord with all of thine heart and lean not to your own understanding." (Pro.3:6)

Prayer;   **"I have come to set captives free."**

_____
_____
_____
_____
_____
_____

Who Will Go?

The lost are uneasy about the church
Not because they believe, God is *not* at work
But, because they know, I am a God for the hurt
My local church, in My community, you have not gone out for Me
The lost and the hurt, know this is not My way. How do they know?
I made them this way. I created mankind, in My image. They crave love
From above. They're lost 'till they find it and you have not offered it
They will not stick around, for fake love to be found
They, already have fake love in their life
Only My real presence, will draw their life
You live like Pharisees! My lost, will not come to Me. Not through you
Only through Me. I must be in you, lukewarm will not do!
Haven't you seen, all they've been through?
They will NOT come to Me…through fake ministry
You see, when the youth of the city start praising Me, it's because, children
It's Me! It's My spirit, drawing. They don't have a monopoly on Me
I show no favoritism. All these years, I've offered you, Me
But, you choose your way. You choose, your knowledge
Over My strength, over My power!
You choose to close, five days a week
You will not go, to the streets, for My lost sheep
You say, you love Me, but you ignore Me
I've made it clear. It's not hard
Go where they are!
Where is your plan? Where is your strategy? Where is your prayer?
Where is your faith? Faith without works, is dead. This is what I've said!
You work for Me? And not go to the street? You stay in. Even build, another
Church. Leave the first community hurt. Now the second hurt. You work for Me?
Where are the lost, you have won? Where is the love, you have shown? You work for
Me? You build buildings. Now, a second mortgage due. When will you do what I said?
Go to the street, and bring in, My lost sheep.
Build for Me, a real love… Ministry

My word teaches you *real* Ministry
Serve the lost. This will bring them to Me

"So God created in mankind His own image..." (Gen. 1:27)

"...I have loved you with an everlasting. love; I have drawn you with unfailing kindness." (Jere. 31:3)

"... I now realize how true it is that God does not show favoritism." (Acts 10:34)

"Record the vision and inscribe it on tablets, that the one who reads it may run. For the vision is yet for the appointed time; It hastens toward the goal and it will not fail..." (Hab. 2:2)

"For I was hungry, and you fed Me. I was thirsty and you gave me a drink, I was a stranger and you invited Me into your home. I was naked, and you gave Me clothing. I was sick, and you cared for Me. I was in prison, and you visited Me." (Mat. 25:35-36)

"Not by might, not by power, but by My spirit..." (Zech. 4:6)

"...Go out to the roads and country lanes and behind the hedges and urge anyone you find to come in, so My house will be full." (Luke 14:23)

Prayer:

_____
_____
_____
_____
_____
_____
_____
_____
_____

Will You Bring the Lost to Me?

We, must build up one another and encourage ourselves
We must stir up our gifts while seeking God's help
Jesus, is the vine. We are His branches
We must stay focused, patiently learning
Keeping our eyes on Jesus, while He grows His fruit in us
Iron sharpens iron. An angry man is not good company
But, this is not meant, to not go and set others free
Guard your spirit. Add to faith, goodness and to
Goodness, knowledge and continue this way
Presenting your body, as a living sacrifice
Living for Jesus and doing what's right
While we are taking care of ourselves
We must love others, as we love our self
So, we as a church, must still offer our help
Care for others. Bring in sisters and brothers
Into the family. Remember Jesus did this for us
It seems, the local church, does not understand
We continue, to not take a stand, in the community
We are living like, It's all about, "What about me?"
Jesus is in the prison, in the hungry, in the sick
We're commanded to stir up our gifts…to "Go"
Sharpening your gifts, will bring you before kings
Stay in school, get your training, lessons and degrees
And with all you do, Jesus says, "Bring the lost to Me"
You don't know the day or the hour, in which I come
In the last days, all will be going about their own ways
And then like a thief in the night, I will crack the sky! What then?
Will My lost children live in a fiery furnace? Crying, gnashing their teeth
Forever burnin'! When will you go out, from the church facility and bring
My lost children to Me! When?

> *Be merciful to those who doubt; save others by*
>
> *snatching them from the fire…"*
>
> *(Jude 1:23)*

My heart is broken. Broken for My children. Separated from Me
Pastor, will you go into the community
And bring My lost to Me?

"But you dear friends, must build each other up in your most holy faith, pray in the power of the Holy Spirit..." (Jude 1:20)

"David strengthened himself in the Lord his God." (Sam. 30:6)

"Which of these do you think was a neighbor to the man who fell into the hands of robbers? The expert in the law replied, 'The one who had mercy on him.' Jesus told him, **'Go and do likewise.'" (Luke 10:37)**

"For you yourselves are fully aware that the day of the Lord will come like a thief in the night." (1 Thess. 5:2)

"In will happen in a moment, in the blink of an eye, when the last trumpet is blown. For when the trumpet sounds, those who have died will be raised to live forever. And we who are living will alsobe transformed." (1 Cor. 15:52)

"And the angels will throw them into the fiery furnace, where there will be weeping and gnashing of teeth." (Mat. 13:42)

"The Lord is not slow keeping His promise... Instead He is patient with you, not wanting anyone to perish, but everyone to come to repentance." (2 Pet. 3:9)

Prayer;

_____

_____

_____

_____

_____

Chapter Seven

"LOCK–UP" … PRISONER OF GOD

- EPHESIANS 3:1

YOU HAVE JESUS CHRIST ON YOUR SIDE!

HE HAS BEEN CALLING YOU A WHILE NOW

WAKE UP, OH SLEEPER - IT'S YOUR TIME!

ARISE!   (EPH. 5:14)

Heart Cry

Prisoner, my sister, my brother, under lock and key, I must tell you, sorry
We as a church, haven't been to check on you. We've strayed, from true
And I got to say, you've been strong and mighty too
I'm making a special prayer book, just for you
Got to tell you, the plans God has for you
See, My Father, is the opposite of us. Did you know, you're his first love?
He says, I didn't come, to call, those who think they're righteous
But, I'm calling ALL sinners. The real winners!
He's got you, in His heart. He's got you, in His hand!
He's the perfect Father. Perfect Brother. He causes you, to stand!
I mean, He is CRAZY for you. Obsessed with you! He is right there, with you!
Where sin is, His grace mightily abounds. Whatever's going on, where you are
You must know, YOU'RE HIS SHINING STAR! Can't have you hopeless, not
Knowing who you are; Unable to recognize, YOU GOT YOUR Father's eyes!
When, I pray for you, my whole heart cries; Right this moment, God sees
Your eyes. If you reached, right now. You'd touch Him, somehow!
They, that worship Him, worship Him in Spirit. He says, I no longer, call you…
Servant. But, I call you my friend, through thick and thin. I'm with you, till the end!
No need to discuss, what you have, *not* done or what you, *have* done
God needs to talk to you. Talk to Him. He's got to interact with you, as a best friend
He is your anointed, Holy Father. Call Him Dad! He's the best, you've ever had
He's like none other, when you need a brother. He's there, right now!
Reach deep, as your heart cries. Embrace Him now! Let Him give you His eyes
Often, there are debates, about his word and about His way, but He is so powerful
He will come, where you are and give you the truth. He says, I send my Holy Spirit
He comes to comfort you and teach you, all things. Don't get caught up, in other
Stuff. He's got His hand, on you. Read, pray, He will give you, insight. He will give
You, His might. He says, I will give you what to say, at the time you need to say it
Satan is not greater! Whatever you think, draw near to God. He will draw near to you
He will teach you all truth. You can have no other God. Now you know, this is true
In a home, can there be two heads? No way! So, it's clear to you. There must be, one
Head. Which is God, The Father, the Son, the Holy Spirit. Any other contradiction is
false. You must Still love, yes. Still watch and pray, yes. Still help others, yes…

But, you cannot partner with, false
This is My word. This is My way. I will show you, as you pray - My Way

"I have not come to call the righteous, but sinners, to repentance." (Luke 5:32)

"Submit yourselves therefore to God. Resist the devil, and he will flee from you. Draw near to God, and he will draw near to you..." (James 4:7-8)

"For as the heavens are higher than the earth, so are my ways higher than your ways and my thoughts than your thoughts." (Is. 55:9)

"What shall we say then? Are we to continue in sin so that grace may increase? By no means! How can we who died to sin still live in it?" (Rom. 6:1-2)

"But the Advocate, the Holy Spirit, whom the Father will send in my name, will teach you all things and will remind you of everything I have said to you." "my peace I give you. I do not give to you as the world gives..." (John 14:26-27)

"But you will receive power when the Holy Spirit comes upon you. And you will be my witnesses..." (Acts 1:8)

"I no longer call you servants, because a servant does not know his master's business. Instead, I have called you my friends..." (John 15:15)

Prayer;

_____

_____

_____

_____

The Only Way

Let me tell you something, son
My heart you have won!
So you think you haven't had a Father
I'm a friend and a Father, that sticks closer
Than a brother. I'm a Friend, Father and Mother
Like no other. My love daily provides for you
My heart daily feeds and nourishes you
My words break every barrier, to save you
I love you, I need you, in relationship with Me
Do, you know son, what a revival is?
It stirs up your heart, and for Me you live
A revival, revives… a heart, that's been livin' lies
A revival makes you survive, this world's enemy
Survive and live your destiny! Survive and live, abundantly!
Stop watching these preachers on TV, and not hearing one word
You're designed to triumph! Son, get in your word. I need to speak to you
Can't you see, I got a job for you? I must come back. I can't leave my children
Behind. Can you hear my hearts cry? Stop believing the lies. I am your Father
My Son is Jesus Christ. In His name, all wrong is made right. In His name, every
Crooked place is made straight. In His name, no lost person, can ever be the same
Evil spirits are cast out, in His name. In His name, sickness cannot stay. In His name
A way is made, where there is, no way. Son, I'm a miracle working God
Son, Jesus Christ, is the way to Me. The only way to Me
Try Me. No, *really* try, Me. Talk to Me
Just, you and Me. I Am here
I Am there, right now
Beside you
Here, to
Guide
you

"Krazy"
You know…
"God is Gracious"

I am you Father. Choose this day,
Whom you will serve. Son, choose Me
My son, choose Me. For *real*, this time

"Jesus said to them, 'If God were your Father, you would love me. For I have come here from God. I have not come on my own, God sent me.'" (John 8:42)

"Here I am! I stand at the door and knock. If anyone hears my voice and opens the door, I will come in and eat with that person, and they with me." (Rev. 3:20)

"Then we will not turn away from you; revive us, and we will call on your name." (Ps. 80:18)

"Create in me a pure heart, Oh God, and renew a steadfast spirit within me." (Ps. 51:10)

"Father to the fatherless, defender of widows-this is God whose dwelling is holy. God places the lonely in families; he sets the prisoners free and gives them joy. But he makes the rebellious live in sun-scorched land." (Ps. 68:5-6)

"I also tell you this: if two of you agree here on earth concernng anything you ask, my Father in heaven will do it for you." (Mat. 18:19)

"'The time has come,' he said. 'The kingdom of God has come near. Repent and believe the good news!'"
(Mark 1:15)

Prayer;

K.K.

_____
_____
_____
_____
_____
_____
_____

Come Work for Me

You have time on your hands, now. Let Me fill you, with wisdom
Not, wisdom from this world, but My wisdom from, My world
You, are living in this world, but you are not of this world
Satan, is the prince of earth. His followers, he is destroying
Killing, stealing from the lost men, women, girls and boys
My, harvest of souls, is plenty! But My laborers are few
Come work with Me. I got your destiny. I got your history
I knew you long before, you were in your mother's womb
It was Me, only Me who knew you. I was with your family
Son, it was Me. I've waited patiently. Time, is running out
You, must come to Me. I have every answer. I have all power
My followers, have denied Me. Seeking, not to mention, My Son
But, he who receives My Son gets Me! Do you see, Satan's strategy?
If, he can get others, to deny my Son, they can NEVER, ever come, to Me
Yes, I forgive! But, do not fall for and believe, that I would give you leaders
That live harshly, live in sin and lie to My church, leading thousands astray
These are false prophets, false teachers. Son, let us sit and reason together
You were made in My image. Yes, Satan has tempted your heart and
Your mind, at one time. But, I am your Father
No matter your circumstance. I speak to you!
Made in My image, you know this is true
It's because you are Mine!
I am your Father.
You are My son.
Work with Me now
For the world
To be won!

My harvest is ready. The laborers are few
I need workers in my vineyard
That are TRUE!

"For the LORD gives wisdom; from His mouth come knowledge and understanding; he stores up sound wisdom for the upright; he is a shield to those who walk in integrity..." (Pro. 2:6-7)

"For we are co-workers in God's service; you are God's field, God's building ...each one should build with care. For no one can lay any foundation other than the one already laid, **which is Jesus Christ." (1 Cor. 9-11)**

"They are not of this world, just as I am not of this world. Sanctify them in the truth; teach them your word, which is truth. As you have sent me into this world, so I have sent them into the world. And for their sake I consecrate myself, that they also may be sanctified in truth. I do not ask for these only, but also for those who will believe in me through their word that they may all be one, just as you, Father, are in me, and I in you, that they may also be in us, so that the world may believe that you have sent me." (John 17:16-21)

"The thief comes only to steal and kill and destroy; I came that they may have life and have it abundantly." (John 10:10)

"...I am the way, and the truth, and the life. No one comes to the Father except through me." (John 14:6)

"...The harvest is plentiful, but the workers are few" (Luke 10:2)

Prayer;

_____

_____

_____

Abba Father

Daughter, there in jail, I love you
Many have let you down. Several in the ground
Can't you see if I remove, the scales from eyes
You're My greatest prize. I smile, when I look in your eyes
You must refuse to walk blindly. I got a pathway straight to Me
That you can, clearly see. 'Babygirl,' you belong to Me
I am your Father. I know you've been rejected, by others
But not Me. I love you tenderly. I give to you, My mercy
I don't hold your sins against you, when you come to Me'
COME TO ME! I'm waiting patiently. You're My Destiny
We're gonna' hang together. Dancin' with, you in My arms
Father and daughter dance. Sound the alarms. Daddy's home
You're not alone. I extend, My hand, My heart, My all to you
I'm the best of friends. Don't you know, I've chosen you
Waiting on you, to choose Me too. I so adore you, I love you
I'm all you need. Come sit with Me, on My knee
You are not alone. I hold you in My arms!
Sound the alarm. Dad is home with you. I've had My eyes on you, a long time
Knocking on your hearts door. I can't wait anymore. You must let Me in, now!
I need to come in your heart's door. Open your heart, your life, your soul
These others, can't help! Can't you see? I must also, set them free
This cursing and fighting, is only inviting, the enemy of your soul
Don't go. Don't go! I'm here. I'm near. I rubbing your head
Feel My breath in your hair. Daughter run to Me. **I am SAFETY**
Safety with your love and care. I'm a safe haven, everywhere
Come live with Me. I'm your Daddy. You're a Daddy's girl
My girl. My world. Choose Me!
I have already chosen…

I have already chosen...
You!

'...I will never leave you nor forsake you..." (Deut. 31:8)

"For everyone who asks receives, and the one who seeks finds and to the one who knocks it will be opened." (Mat. 7:8)

"Immediately, something like scales fell from Saul's eyes, and he could see again. He got up and was baptized..." (Acts 9:18)

"No one born of God makes a practice of sinning, for God's seed abides in him, and he cannot keep on sinning because he has been born of God." (1 John 3:9)

"So you have not received a spirit that makes you fearful slaves. Instead, you received God's Spirit when he adopted you as his own children. Now we call him, "Abba Father."
(Rom. 8:15)
"...The Lord is my helper; I will not be afraid..." (Heb. 13:6)

"What then shall we say to these things? If God is for us, who can be against us? (Rom. 8:31)

"The LORD is for me, so I will have no fear. What can mere people do to me? (Ps. 118:6)

"Choose today whom you will serve..." (Josh. 24:15)

Prayer;   **- Jesus, teach me how, You love me...**

_____
_____
_____
_____
_____
_____

He Hears you

Family, now listen to me
You know, in your heart
What is right, what is not
You know, what is good care of you
You know, what is bad treatment of you
I got something to say to you. My sister, my brother
God hears you! Get His attention. Explain your situation
Yes, the bible says, He knows all things, that you need
He also says, let all your request, be made known to Him
This may, be so you know, you told your very best friend
…Him!
Be anxious for nothing and in prayer, make your request
Known to Him. My brother, my sister, I got to talk to you
I've seen, so many miracles, it's true. Let me talk to you
God's Holy Spirit, will lead you! Will teach you all things
Jesus Christ, is the same. Never changes. Will never change
You, must believe! God sent His Son, to die for you and me
He gave His life, in a brutal death, on the cross of Calvary…
He rose three day later, with all power over death in His hands
Whatever He says, stands! Death and life, have no power over Him
He answers prayer. You are aware! He's deeply concerned, you know
Not like some of these, 'church' folk, though. Leaving you alone and weak
Your pain so deep. Family cryin'. Brothers and sisters dyin'. They dancin'
yet… SLEEP!
See, Jesus is not like that! That's a fact! Don't judge Him, on their misery
Some, have tunnel vision, "me, me, me". Don't judge Jesus, on their greed!
Get out your bible! Read! Ask Jesus, "Please speak to me." He will teach you
Give you visions. Speak to you in dreams. Jesus can handle…
Your "ANYTHING!"
He is calling you, Loud and clear. Got your name, in my ear…

Give Jesus your Heart
Right now, He is near. Have no fear
With Him, all things are possible!

"Don't worry about anything; instead pray about everything. Tell God what you need, and thank him for all he has done."
(Phil. 4:6)

"You, however, are not in the flesh but in the Spirit, if in fact the Spirit of God dwells in you. Anyone that does not have the Spirit of Christ does not belong to him." (Rom. 8:9)

"But, the Helper, the Holy Spirit, whom the Father will send in my name, he will teach you all things and bring to your remembrance all that I have said to you."   (John 14:26)

"Watch out for those dogs, those evildoers, those mutilators of the flesh." (Phil. 3:2)

"They are dogs with mighty appetites; they never have enough. They are shepherds who lack understanding; they all turn to their own way, they seek their own gain." (Is. 56:11)

"Let the wicked change their ways and banish the very thought of doing wrong. Let them turn to the LORD that he may have mercy on them. Yes, turn to our God, for
he will forgive generously." (Is. 55:7)

Prayer;

_____

_____

_____

_____

_____

_____

_____

Peace and Strength unto you - I

Prisoner, can I please appeal to you
You are my sister and my brother
Please, to your own self be true
I so miss you and pray for you
I need you to be strong
Whatever's happened to your mind
Over, an extended part of time
I speak right now, to fill your heart
With an enduring, faithful part
A courageous kind of love
Given only from above
It's a supernatural love
Causes you to forgive others, as well as yourself
You may not have had, good help
You, may have been totally led astray
And wish often, you had gone another way
But, I need you to be compassionate and strong
I need you to renew your heart and mind, to think
A mind stayed on Thee, is kept in constant peace
Please, listen close to me. You are loved tenderly
More than you know. Out here, tension grows
But you, you right there, you are a masterpiece!
And though you are hurting, out here, we are praying
We have not forgotten your pain. I pray daily for your gain
Gain strength and endurance, for your time. Gain a healthy state of mind
You can't do that, if you focus on the bad. Get your mind on, the glad!
What, is your body? It belongs to God. Everything you need, He's got
Trust me, when I tell you. Miracles, in you, He will do. I pray right now
A miracle for you!
New body, soul and mind. Blessings all the time. His love, I pray for you
You are not alone
He holds you in His palms. He is in control. With you everywhere you go

"You, keep him in perfect peace whose mind is stayed on you because he, trusts in you."

(Is. 26:3)

Peace and strength be unto you this day
In Jesus Mighty Miraculous Powerful and Holy Name!

"I appeal to you therefore, brothers, by the mercies of God, to present your bodies as a living sacrifice, holy and acceptable to God, which is your spiritual worship." (Rom. 12:1)

"Be on your guard; stand firm in the faith; be courageous; be strong." (1 Cor. 16:13)

"Endure suffering along with me, as a good soldier of Jesus Christ." (2 Tim. 2:3)

"God blesses those who patiently endure testing and temptation. Afterward they will receive the crown of life that God promised to those who love him." (James 1:12)

"'...Love the Lord your God with all your heart and with all your soul and with all your strength and with all your mind.' And, 'Love your neighbor as yourself.'" (Luke 10:27)

"...the LORD your God goes with you; he will never leave you nor forsake you." (Deut. 31:6)

"I pray that out of his glorious riches he may strengthen you with power through his Spirit in your inner being." (Eph. 3:16)

"Finally be strong in the Lord and in his mighty power." (Eph. 6:10)

Prayer;

_____

_____

_____

Peace and Strength unto you - II

The Joy of the Lord
Is your strength, your only strength!
I pray for you, laughter. I pray for you, joy
Joy that flows over, till your cup runs over
Laughter does the heart good, like medicine
Laughter makes me, so happy to see
I picture you now, laughing somehow
I picture you now, with an abundance somehow
Anything bad, give it to God, in Jesus Christ name
My loved one, you will never be the same!
I pray for you, living water, living inside
As the Holy Spirit guides, every step inside
Every step your heart takes. Every decision, your mind makes
You are full of Joy! Full of laughter! Full of Peace! Full of Strength!
My heart leaps for joy, as I pray this in the Spirit of the Lord
For I know, nothing can ever be more, than the Spirit of the Lord
He hears this prayer for you! You should be now, rejuvenated too
Just have faith. That means, believing without physically seeing
Put on your spiritual eyes. Allow your Father, to give you, His eyes
Reach for Him. Believe in your heart now. God I believe, your Son died
                              …for ME!
Just for me! And three days later arose with all power in His hand
Right this minute, He causes me to stand! Stand strong. Stand long!
I draw near to Him. He draws near to me, unbelievably, but I believe!
I have this Faith in God, through Jesus Christ His Son! Nothing else matters
                    My Heart He has won!
Now you must promise me, you will read your bible. You will study
And the Holy Spirit will lead you. Teach you. Guide you. Comfort you
Trust Jesus, for the Holy Spirit to bring everything back to your memory
He will do this for you. My sister, my brother…

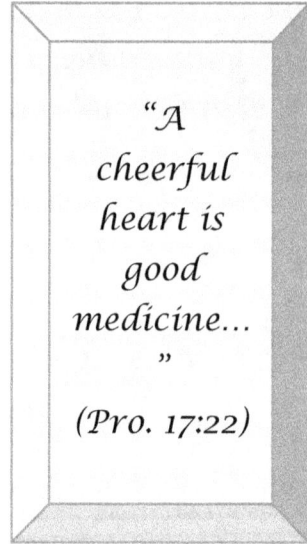

"A cheerful heart is good medicine…"

(Pro. 17:22)

To your own self be, true!
Jesus is the Best Father, Brother, Friend
The greatest life decision. – Jesus and you. - Amen

"...And do not be grieved, for the joy of the LORD is your strength." (Neh. 8:10)

"A man's spirit will endure sickness, but who can bear a crushed spirit?" (Pro. 18:14)

"Whoever loves his life will lose it, and whoever hates his life in this world will keep it for eternal life." (John 12:25)

"...his delight is in the law of the LORD; and in his law doeth he meditate day and night... And he shall be like a tree planted by the rivers of water, that bringeth forth his fruit in his season; his leaf shall not wither; and whatsoever he doeth shall prosper." (Ps. 1:2-3)

"...Do not let your hearts be troubled and do not be afraid." (John 14:27)

"for the Holy Spirit will teach you at that time what you should say." (Luke 12:12)

"For it is not you who will be speaking—it will be the Spirit of your Father speaking through you." (Mat. 10:20)

"Now go; I will help you speak and will teach you what to say." (Ex. 4:12)

Prayer;

_____

_____

_____

_____

Love Rises in you

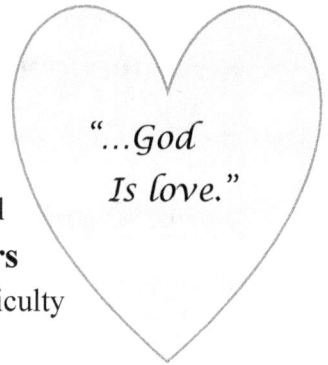

"...God Is love."

Lord, what do you need me to cover…
Sister and brother, love one another! God's love is powerful
This is how Jesus uses you! Love beyond barriers
Love beyond race. Love beyond religion. Love beyond difficulty
Love beyond bars!
You, can start a ministry, in prison. Start with prayer and bible study
Just need two or three. It will grow, cause that's what God's love does
It grows. Sorta' like wild flowers. Sorta' like a waterfall. Rushing over, all
Your love, will be tested. Seek the Lord with prayer, faithfulness and fasting
Ask Him to speak to you. Listen, when He does. He, will fill you with His love
Love covers a multitude of sin. Love bears up, under anything and everything
Nothing can hold down love. God's love rises above all else
Read your bible, study His word. He, will use your blessed voice, to be heard
He needs willing vessels and He needs you! You'll be amazed at what He'll do
Write a vision of what your heart desires. List all your passions, filled with fire
This is a talent, He's given you. Floods your heart, this love, He instilled in you
Pray about it. Think it through. Write it down. This Godly dream inside of you
Pray, read and study. Write it all down. Jesus, is totally turning things around!
Be faithful in small things. Keep a song in your heart and sing. Sing His praises
Be thankful in all things. Pray always. Live, dream and believe. Think and seek
Have no time for carnal talk, which means any ugly thing, not glorifying God
Guard your heart! Keep it for the King! Each day, give yourself totally, to Him
Focus on Him! His power is amazing! Almighty, He is! Now in you, He lives!
This power, is too much to contain. So, guard it well, your life, your blessing
Ask for the Chaplain, he can pray. Attend, the church meetings, on Sunday
Or, any day the schedule offers. Get the training, that you want and need
God has given you everything to succeed. The Holy Spirit, will teach you
Love and forgive. God will use you! Keep a journal, of His work in you
He's about to mightily use you! The world needs, what you have
Share your testimony, with all those around you
Give Jesus, the glory in everything you do…

Godly wisdom and Magnificent Love
Will abound Bountifully, in you!

"...Love your neighbor as yourself..." (Mark 12:31)

"Love is patient and kind; love does not envy or boast; it is not arrogant or rude. It does not insist on its own way; it is not irritable or resentful; it does not rejoice in wrong doing, but rejoices in the truth. Love bears all things, believes all things, hopes all things, endures all things."
"Loves bears up under anything and everything that comes..."
(1 Cor. 13:7)

"Consider it pure joy, my brothers and sisters, whenever you face trials of many kinds, because you know that the testing of your faith produces perseverance." (James 1:3)

"If you only knew the gift God has for you and who you are speaking to, you would ask me, and I would give you living water." (John 4:10)

"...You have been faithful with a few things; I will put you in charge of many things..." (Mat. 25:23)

"For where two or three gather in my name, there I am with them." (Mat. 18:20)

"Above all, keep loving one another earnestly, since love covers a multitude of sin." (1 Pet. 4:8)

Prayer;

_____

_____

_____

_____

Flyin' High

I have started this new way
When I stumble
Help me Lord Jesus, to pray
I must not, get caught up
In this evil world
I'm a new creature
Built just for you
I cannot turn back
No matter what, I do
I'm 100% committed to You
You, have chosen me
And I have answered you
My answer is yes, Lord, yes
I will walk in faith, toward You
Hold me close, and never let me go
I'm attached to You and You to me
Unmatched, is Your love for me
I thrive in Your word, daily
I am the fruit, on Your vine
Jesus, mold me, in Your time
I patiently wait for You
I'm an eagle in Your nest
Daily getting stronger
To pass every test!
I will endure until the end
Victory is promised, to be mine!
I walk the walk. Talk the talk
My life no longer, mine...

"*I'm a new creature in Christ.*"
2 Cor. 5:17

"*Cast your cares on the LORD and he will sustain you; he will NEVER let the righteous be shaken.*"
(*Ps.* 55:22)

"*Cast all your anxiety on him because he cares for you*"
(1 *Pet.*5:7)

Jesus,
I soar like an Eagle, in Your kingdom

"Seek his will in all you do, and he will show you which path to take." (Pro. 3:6)

"...those who hope in the LORD will renew their strength. They will soar on wings like eagles; they will run and not grow weary, they will walk and not be faint." (Is. 40:31)

"if anyone would come after me, let him deny himself and take up his cross and follow me." (Mat. 16:24)

"Commit everything you do to the LORD. Trust him, and he will help you." (Ps. 37:5)

"And after you have suffered a little while, the God of grace, who has called you to his eternal glory in Christ, will himself restore, confirm, strengthen, and establish you," (1 Pet. 5:10)

"for you know that when your faith has been tested, your endurance has a chance to grow." (James 1:3)

"...the cares of this world and the deceitfulness of riches and the desire for other things...choke the word ..." (Mark 4:19)

"Commit your work to the LORD, and your plans will be established." (Pro. 16:3)

Prayer;

_____

_____

_____

_____

_____

_____

_____

They Call Me, J E S U S

Sons and daughters, inside those four walls, behind 'them' bars
You, are so very blessed! You just need to know, who's you are
I'm speaking for My Father. He says, I'm an ambassador for Him
He says, to tell you, "Your heart, He desperately **seeks** to win."
I, don't know your life story. I don't know your losses, or gains
I have no clue, of your childhood or your deep drenching pain
I don't know, 'bout all these preachers. But you are my concern
God will handle them. All I know, is for you, His heart burns!
If you don't begin to read your bible, you've lost, at survival
These wolves are mixing lies with truth. God is seeking…YOU!
Seeking, 'till it pains His heart. Seeking, 'till He can't live apart
From you. He MUST have you. He can't bare life without you
He, has sent his children for you, sent the shepherds too
But, you know this life well. Not much, anyone could sell, you
You, see what's happening. God has made it clear, have no fear
He has ordained a time such as this, to basically square up His list
He is NOT tryin' to lose you. He needs a voice, to reach you. Here it is!
So, you think you just picked up, any old book. No, take a deeper look!
God of the universe, made and molded you. Knows all your joy and hurt
He has sent out a clarion call. I got to reach you ALL! I got to reach you
We can, no longer depend on the preacher, to teach ya! Get your bible
Pray for revival! Pray, against that wolf and false spirit. Submit to God
That evil will flee. Trust in His word. You will live and not die! Trust Me
When God sends you a personal book. You need to take a second look!
Take a real look. Close your eyes or look at the sky. Take a deeper look
Ask Him, "Are You there, somewhere?"- "Would You help me, in here?"
Meditate. Give Him your time. His words say, "I want to sup with you
Dine with, you. I need time with, you. My Holy Spirit will fill and teach you
Teach you, all things, bring back to your remembrance, all and everything!"
Give Jesus a chance, for REAl! Let me tell you, HE'S REAL! He will wake you
He will give you a visions and make your dreams live again! In real brilliance
You will come forth, with visions and plans! You've just begun! Now STAND!

I have created the heaven's and the earth
And I have known you since before birth. - Jesus

"In the beginning, God created the heavens and the earth."
(Gen. 1:1)

"in the last days, God says, I will pour out my Spirit on all people. Your sons and daughters will prophesy, your young men will see visions, your old men will dream dreams." (Acts 2:17)

"When the Father sends the Advocate as my representative— that is, the Holy Spirit—he will teach you everything and remind you of everything I have told you." (John 14:26)

"...If you hear my voice and open the door, I will come in, and we will share a meal together as friends." (Rev. 3;20)

"...You are the Christ, the Son of the living God." (Mat. 16:16)

Submit yourselves therefore to God. Resist the devil, and he will flee from you."
(James 4:7)

"Before I formed you in the womb I knew you, before you were born I set you apart; I appointed you as a prophet to the nations."
(Jeremiah 1:5)

Dedicated to Jeremy Scott
- Appointed by God

Prayer;

_____

_____

_____

_____

_____

_____

_____

Chapter Eight

SINNER COME HOME

- JOHN 3:16

WHY DO YOU HIDE FROM ME?
I HAVE BEEN CALLING YOU
I AM GOD - YOUR FATHER
COME HOME

No Excuse

Sinner, you have no excuse
Stop blaming everyone
Stop blaming anyone
Haven't you been told
The greatest story of old
God loves you, adores you
Sent His Son, to die for you
He rose for you, It's true
His heart, daily aches for you
He sees how you live
He is begging to forgive
He needs you, to ask Him to
He doesn't push His way, on you
Don't you think, you need Him
He's a Father, brother and a friend
Haven't you believed, any testimony
And seen another, giving Him glory
Stop acting, like you really don't know
And, No blaming, these fake preachers though
Cause you won't answer the call. And you know, God created all!
See, God has this special plan. And He needs us all, and needs you now to stand
Are you one that chooses drugs? And give your friends and family 'them' fake hugs?
Nothin' real, 'bout lettin' friends drive drunk. Nothin' real, 'bout being Satan's punk
If you live your life, for that liar. You'll burn in, his eternal, blazin' fire
Satan, got them fake preachers in on it to. He desperately seeks you
You have no excuse. Satan comes to steal, kill and destroy
God has come to fill your life, with abundant joy
Choose this day. Jesus Christ is the only way!
He wants you. Can He trust you?

> "...but there is a
> friend who sticks
> closer than a
> brother."
>
> (Pro. 18:24)

You have no, excuse!
Jesus Christ is calling you!

> *"For ever since the world was created, people have seen the earth and sky. Through everything God made, they can clearly see his invisible qualities- his eternal power and divine nature. So they have no excuse for not knowing God."*
> *(Romans 1:20)*

"For God so loved the world, that he gave his only Son, that whoever believes in him should not perish but have eternal life."
(John 3;16)

"Jesus answered, "I am the way and the truth and the life..."
(John 14:16)

Prayer;   **Jesus, open my eyes to see, through Your eyes...**

_____
_____
_____
_____
_____
_____
_____
_____
_____
_____
_____
_____
_____

I Am the Way, the Truth & the Life

It just seems to me
You think, livin' for Christ, is corny
You've been tainted by these phonies
That, is Satan's plan
These fakers don't stand
Jesus is like an earthquake
His power makes you shake
Makes you walk true, not fake
An example for righteousness
An example of tenderness
An example to pass life's test
An example of a life that's blessed
God is fire
He's got power!
So knowledgeable
He trembles in your soul
Goes with you, where you go
When we take Him, to the street
He heals the sick, sets men free. A powerful God
Interested in *who* you are. He's interested in *how* you are
You think, He's like these preachers, just sitting around, living large?
How twisted you are. He's a life changing God! He wants to change who you are
He came to earth, as your living sacrifice. Start a real, 'church' or a bible study night
Show others, you're living in the past. And don't get started and then get side
Tracked. Ending up, just taking care of only, 'you'!
That's what these, phonies do
Give yourself to Christ, then GO
Go and save a lost person's life
Jesus died for you…

> *"So do not fear, for I am with you; do not be dismayed, for I am your God. I will strengthen you and help you."*
>
> *(Is. 41:10)*

Your holy sacrifice
The Way, the Truth and the Life

> *Jesus answered, "I am the way and the truth and the life..." (John 14:16)*

"... the LORD is the true God; he is the living God and the everlasting King. At his wrath the earth quakes, and the nations cannot endure his indignation." (Jere. 10:10)

"For the LORD your God is he who goes with you to fight for you against your enemies, to give you the victory." (Deut. 20:4)

"Consider it joy, my brothers and sisters, whenever you face trials of many kinds, because you know that the testing of your faith produces perseverance." (James 1:3)

"Sin will be rampant everywhere, and the love of many will grow cold. But the one who endures till the end will be saved." (Mat. 24:13)

"But he knows the way that I take; when he has tested me, I will come forth as gold." (Job 23:10)

Prayer;   **Jesus, be with me right where I am...**

_____

_____

_____

_____

_____

_____

_____

_____

_____

I will Mightily use you, Love Jesus

Sinner…I'm crying for you
I see what's happening
I see the scales over your eyes
The confusion and lies
Satan, is the prince of the earth
His plan is to destroy you, first
Before you choose, new birth
Unless, a man is born again
He cannot enter God's Kingdom
You must, give your life to Jesus
He cares greatly for you
Works, 'them' miracles too
It's, Satan's lies, feeding you lies!
You need a substance to get high?
You got to sell your body, on the side?
He is feeding you, that you ain't worth much
He is feeding you, you need his filthy, evil touch
And, that you got to live like a whore. Baby, no more!
You, don't have to sell yourself short. And always, to evil resort
I'm, trying to tell you, Satan is a liar! He's got planned for you, that eternal fire
But Christ, wants to breathe into you, His contagious fire! Your heart's desire
These false prophets, false teachers, wolves, liars, NOT speaking the truth
God's trying to, BIG time, advance you! You are the one He wants to use!
Don't let anyone, lie to you. You must live holy, through His power!
They don't know how to preach that. Cause they haven't done that!
'They' fake. Give up your excuse
You got no excuse…

Allow God to mightily use you!
He is raising up an army to go win His lost
He is Seeking you out, now!

"I am leaving you with a gift- peace of mind and heart. And the peace I give is a gift the world cannot give. So don't be troubled or afraid." (John 14:27)

"For the prince of this world is coming. He has no hold over me..." (John 14:31)

"For God is not a God of confusion but of peace..." (1 Cor. 14:33)

"You keep in perfect peace whose mind is stayed on you,because he trusts in you." (Is. 26:3)

"Jesus replied, 'I tell you the truth, unless you are born again, you cannot see the Kingdom of God.'"
(John 3:3)

"For God has not given us a spirit of fear and timidity, but of power, love, and self-discipline." (2 Tim. 1:7)

"Delight yourself in the Lord, and he will give you the desires of your heart." (Psalm 37:4)

Prayer;   **Lord, teach me on this path to recognize you...**

_____

_____

_____

_____

_____

_____

_____

_____

No Way to Our Father, except through, His Son

They got this new, yet old thing out
Says, tell everyone, they're a King
This, is a true statement
Because God is King
And we are made in His image
However, it is also true
We, turned away
And became sinners too
If, we don't acknowledge this
It's another one of Satan's tricks
See, before Adam and Eve sinned
Satan told them, they "would be just like God."
So, Eve was enticed, by desiring to be just like God
Yes, we are, just like God
But, we were separated from Him
This is HUGE, and cannot be diminished
While separated from Him
We, were unable to touch Him, or 'be like Him'
So, God sent His Son, His only begotten Son
To live and die, a tragic death, on earth
After an amazing and miraculous birth
So, we could experience rebirth
He suffered great pain
Because, for you and me, He came!
These preachers are starting to leave this out
Don't fall for the hype. God sent His Son, Jesus Christ
That, we would have eternal life. Life in heaven. Reigning with Jesus, forever
Run, if they diminish the name of Jesus Christ. Satan wants to lessen, His name
Because there is no way to the Father, except through, the Son
If they don't lift up, the name of Jesus…Run!

> "My little children, I am writing these things to you so that you will not sin. But if anyone does sin, we have an advocate with the Father, Jesus Christ the righteous."
> (1 John 2:1)

Jesus, is NOT a mere 'pathway.'
He is
'THE' WAY, THE TRUTH AND THE LIFE!

"I am the way, the truth and the life." (John 14:6)

"For all have sinned and fall short of the glory of God..."
(Rom. 3:23)

"For God so loved the world, He gave His only begotten Son, that whoever believes in him shall not perish but..."
(John 3:16)

"The angel replied, "The Holy Spirit will come upon you, and the power of the Most High will overshadow you. So the baby to be born will be holy, and he will be called the Son of God."
(Luke 1:35)

"He himself bore our sins in his body on the tree, that we might die to sin and live to righteousness. By his wounds you have been healed." (1 Pet. 2:24)

"So Christ was sacrificed once to take away the sins of many; and he will appear a second time, not to bear sin, but to bring salvation to those who are waiting for him." (Heb. 9:28)

"...No one can come through the Father except through me."
(John 14:6)

"...for they do not know the voice of strangers." (John 10:5)

Prayer;   Jesus, open my ears to hear your voice calling me...

_____

_____

_____

_____

_____

The Last Days Have Come

Oh sinner…Precious child of God
You got to wake up! And give Heaven a call
Cry out to God's Son
It's God's tender, heart you have won!
You got to wake up and learn what to look for
You're gettin' tricked and deceived
It's a spiritual warfare, out here
Satan is taking it, way more serious
He knows he is about to lose, all of us!
He has blinded, the very elite of God
He has twisted, the words of God
He has weakened, even the strong
But, make no mistake, God is still in control
Lots of preachers, can't get you to Him anymore
Too many, living like a whore
Sold out to demons at their door!
You got to wake up sinner! You know it's time!
God has blessed you in your body, soul and mind
One thing about you, you're not trying to waste time
When a sinner, gets on fire for God, he's sold out
A sinner, on fire for God is not filled with doubt
He knows God will do, exactly what He has said
Heal the sick, cast out evil spirits, raise the dead!
When JESUS changes you, He'll speak a testimony through you
He'll give you fire and speak to you, His hearts' desire. All you need to do is pray
Study your bible. Get a few friends, sold out to revival. Read, pray, fast and get
Strong. Jesus will stand in you strong. Your hands have healing power!
Go, lay them on the sick. Ask God, to please anoint you, quick!
For such a time as this. The world is lying, dying and sick
You must study His word. His voice, through you
Must be heard…

**I promised in the last days
My sons and daughters, will prophesy
The Last Days Are Now
- Jesus**

"In the last days, God says, I will pour out my Spirit on all people. Your sons and daughters will prophesy, your young men will see visions, your old men will dream dreams." (Acts 2:17)

"For false messiahs and false prophets will appear and perform great signs and wonders to deceive, if possible, even the elect." (Mat. 24:24)

"Watch and pray that you will not fall into temptation. The spirit is willing, but the flesh is weak." (Mat. 26:41)

"...Be a good worker, one who does not need to be ashamed and who correctly explains the word of truth." (2 Tim. 2:15)

"All authority in heaven and on earth has been given to me. Go therefore and make disciples of all nations, baptizing them in the name of the Father and of the Son and of the Holy Spirit, teaching them to observe all that I have commanded you. And behold, I am with you always, to the end of the age." (Mat. 28:18-20)

Prayer;   Jesus, live strong in my heart and use me, Lord…

_____
_____
_____
_____
_____
_____
_____
_____
_____
_____
_____

Choose Me this Day

Sinner come home
I beg you to come home
Our Father is waiting, for you
His heart. His arms open wide
Patiently waiting, to guide you
He says, I've not sent My Son back
Because I'm waiting for you, to come back
Come back to Me. I need you free!
We got to live together, in eternity!
Please come follow Me
Please come back to Me
You have been, off track a while
I've kept you in my arms, that's My style
I'm a loving, Holy God, a merciful Father
I can't live without my sons and daughters!
With, out stretched arms
Reaching for your hand, I stand
Knocking at your heart's door!
Preachers keep preachin', I'm happy
You think I'm happy, concerning losing you?
Each day, I want to talk to you. I wait for you to talk to me
I patiently wait for you. But I need someone, to tell you the truth!
I'm not sittin' here laughing. My daughters are cryin', their sons are dyin'
Some of these speakers, so trifflin'! Telling my children, I'm always laughin'
I'm always smilin', you lyin'. Satan doesn't want anyone to know, I hurt for you
Cause' if My children really knew my heart, they would come for you
They don't know Me. But, I'm raising up an army!
A generation to come for you
To run, and snatch you
From the enemy…

Get ready!

Choose Me!

178

"All those the Father gives me will come to me, and whoever comes to me, I will never drive away." (John 6:37)

"...He does not want anyone to be destroyed, but wants everyone to repent." (2 Pet. 3:9)

"... do not grieve the Holy Spirit of God." (Eph. 4:30)

"...choose for yourselves this day whom you will serve..." (Josh. 24:15)

"...To all who did receive him, who believed in his name, he gave the right to become children of God, who were born, not of blood nor of the will of the flesh nor of the will of man, but of God." (John 1:12-13)

Prayer;   **Jesus, I want to live like your child...**

_____
_____
_____
_____
_____
_____
_____
_____
_____
_____
_____
_____
_____
_____
_____

God Is Not Willing that Anyone Perish

You might be on drugs
You might be selling drugs
Maybe both
Let me give you hope!
Nobody is better than you!
See, Jesus is the opposite of us
Kinda' does things
You may say, a little backwards
Like, the first, shall be last
And the last, shall be first
He seeks out the lost and the deprived
Searches the heart with spiritual eyes
He doesn't look for the perfect, like us
But, takes the imperfect and uses us
He pays everyone the same
No favoritism in His game
He doesn't have a son
He prefers over another
He doesn't have a daughter
He cherishes over the other
He's a perfect Dad. Best you'll ever have. His promises, are for all
Short. Fat, skinny, tall. We think, certain others have arrived
Because these folk stay in the sanctuary and don't come outside
But, this is not the way of Christ! We, are all so precious in His sight!
He can change your life, in just one touch! Like, Saul on the road to Damascus
Overnight, He will use you mightily. to save the sinners and set captives free
He requires you, to live holy and available, for Him. So many others, are just
Not able. They have chosen to live their life, fast. So, when He needs them
They choose His work, last. So, be as Saul and live your life like Paul
When Jesus needs you, Go…

> *"Make every effort to enter through the narrow door, because many, I tell you, will try to enter and will not be able to."*
> *(Luke 13:24)*

He needs you now, you know

He is not willing that any would perish!

"The Lord is not slow to fulfill his promise as some count slowness, but is patient toward you, not wishing that any should perish, but that all should come to repentance."
(2 Pet. 3:9)

"...The hour has come for you to wake up from your slumber, for our salvation is nearer now than when we first believed."
(Rom. 13:11)

"...I now realize how true it is that God does not show favoritism..."
(Acts 10:34

"So the last will be first, and the first will be last."
(Mat. 20:16)

Prayer;   **Jesus, give me that rare, holy fire for you...**

_____
_____
_____
_____
_____
_____
_____
_____
_____
_____
_____
_____
_____

I Stand at your Heart's Door and Knock

Oh Sinner, come home
Please don't follow what you see
I need you to come to Me
I've been knocking at your heart's door
Knowing you want more
You desire a powerful life
One that makes you stand upright
I am your Answer!
I have been waiting a while
Wanting to talk to you, my child
I have big plans for you
Instilling dreams in you
You can't imagine Me with you
I am your greatest dream
Your best cake and ice cream
Been longing for you. everyday
I will take you, in any way, any condition
Did I mention, I miss you so
You, you reading this
Give your heart to Me
Completely. Learn of Me
I will reward you with peace
Your decision will be complete
I will guide you, with Me. Give your heart to Me
Pray for a church to go to. Get baptized. Study and get strong
Take hold of my mighty arm. I am your answer to all that is wrong…
I AM Jesus!

> *"Peace I leave with you; my peace I give to you. I do not give to you as the world gives. Do not let your hearts be troubled and do not be afraid."*
>
> *(John 14:27)*

**…Sinner, Come Home
I am your Father. Are you ready?
I'm waiting for you, now!**

"Behold I stand at the door and knock.
If anyone hears my voice and opens
the door, I will come in to him and
eat with him and he with me."
(Rev. 3:20)

"...Truly, truly, I tell you, I am the gate for the sheep...If anyone
enters through Me, he will be saved. He will come in and
go out and find pasture."
(John 10:7-9)

Prayer;   **Father, I want a real relationship with You...**

_____

_____

_____

_____

_____

_____

_____

_____

_____

_____

_____

_____

_____

_____

_____

_____

Choose Me Above All Else

Oh, how I need to hear from you
I'm sending My power, to move you
Reach for Me. Draw near to Me
I promise, to draw near to you
There is nothing, I cannot do
Trust Me, literally. I am He
I Am, creator of the universe
Won't you give Me your hand
Take the time to understand
I hold the world in My hand! I bleed for you
I believe for you. I died for you. I cry for you
Choose Me. My Father waits to send Me
He can't lose you, in forever, with Me
He wants you. I want you. We are calling you! We are One!
My Holy Spirit will guide you. No need to fear, I am right here. I know you!
From before your mother's womb. And I have known all your wounds
Every injury, every nightmare. I was there. Offering my care…**Choose Me.**
You can't be fake. For that, it's too late. I need real. Just like you need real
I need real. We're related, can't you tell? I need you, as well. Go to work for
Me! My pay is great! I make no mistakes. Yes, there will be heartaches
Heart breaks, trials come to make you strong
With Me, you will have the best life, ever!
I will leave you, NEVER! I stand at your hearts door
Pleading with you, begging you, to let Me come in!
I am your deepest, truest, closest Friend…

> *"Draw near to me and I will draw near to you."*
>
> *(James 4:8)*

Choose Me!

"Before I formed you in the womb I knew you,
before you were born I set you apart; I appointed
you as a prophet to the nations." (Jer. 1:5)

"…Choose you
this day whom
you will serve…."
(Josh. 24:15)

Prayer;

_____

_____

_____

_____

_____

_____

_____

_____

_____

_____

_____

_____

_____

_____

_____

_____

_____

Though my Sins, Were as Scarlet...

I believe you are God's Son
Come into my heart
That you have won
Cleanse me, deep down
Turn, my life around
I believe, You, died on the cross
That I would not be, forever lost
I cannot stay lost
So I give my heart to You
Take it, mold me like You
Made in Your image, I am
Make me like the great, 'I AM'
You are the beginning and end
   'I AM THAT I AM'
Make me over again. I give you
My heart, mind and soul
Take complete control
Go with me, wherever I go
Baptism, in water in next
Baptism in the Holy Spirit, a gift
It comforts, guides and teaches me
I need all of Thee
Father, Son and Holy Ghost
Jesus, send your Spirit now, to teach me the most
I need to be directed by You. I give all of me to You
Lord Jesus, make me brand new…

> *"But the fruit of the Spirit is love, joy, peace, patience, kindness, goodness, faithfulness gentleness, and self-control…"*
>
> *(Gal. 5:22-23)*

**Take my sins Lord and make them white as snow…
Give me now, a new soul. Thank you, Lord!
You Have Made Them White as Snow
Thank you, Lord!**

"... to all who did receive him, to those
who believed in his name, he gave the right to
become children of God."
(John 1:12)

"'Come now, let us settle the matter,' says the LORD. 'Though
your sins are like scarlet, I will make them as white as snow.
Though, they are red like crimson, I will make them
as white as wool.'" (Is. 1:18)

"For God so loved the world that he gave his one and only Son,
that whoever believes in him shall not perish but have
eternal life." (John 3:16)

Prayer;   **Jesus, THANK YOU for coming into my heart...**

_____

_____

_____

_____

_____

_____

_____

_____

_____

_____

_____

_____

_____

_____

_____

_____

Chapter Nine

PARENT OF A LOST CHILD

ISAIAH 40:31

TRUST ME WITH YOUR CHILD! TRUST ME

Parent of a Lost Child

Parent of a lost child
It may have been a while
But, I must convince you
Jesus, is STILL the only truth
Remain with your faith in Him
Pray, with all your heart to Him
Don't let any person sidetrack you
Continue to pray, your child through
Anoint and bless their hands and head
Pray, as you think, resting in your bed
Pray as they, walk and talk
Plead with Jesus. Trust all He says
Parent of a lost child
It may have been awhile
But, don't you dare give up
Give Jesus Christ, all of your trust
Put, teaching and gospel music on
Concentrate, on the worship songs
Believe in your heart, mind and soul
That God maintains complete control
God's about to change, their heart
With a physically visual, new start
No matter, the future, present or past
Jesus is Alpha and Omega. The First and the Last
Mother of a lost child, praying, a long while
We cannot give up. The key, is to trust!
Trust and obey. Whatever our Lord has to say
Faith comes by hearing. Keep hearing God's word
Play the scriptures on cd. Get someone, and touch and agree
Say, God's about to do this for me! You must trust and clearly, see…

Remember faith is when you see, what your heart must believe…

BELIEVE

"...faith comes from hearing, and hearing from the word of Christ." (Rom. 10:17)

"...does God give you the Holy Spirit and work miracles among you because you obey the law? Of course not! It is because you believe the message you heard about Christ." (Gal. 3:5)

"My ears had heard of you but now my eyes have seen you." (Job 42:5)

"Trust in the LORD with all your heart, and do not lean on your own understanding. In all your ways acknowledge Him, and he will make straight your paths." (Pro. 3:5-6)

"...If two of you agree on earth about anything they ask, it will be done for them by my Father in heaven." (Mat. 18:19)

"If you remain in me and my words remain in you, ask whatever you wish, and it will be done for you." (John 15:7)

"For I am not ashamed of the gospel, for it is the power of God for salvation to everyone who believes..." (Rom. 1:6)

Prayer;

_____

_____

_____

_____

_____

_____

_____

Mother of a Lost Child

Talk to Me a while
I so care about you
Desire, to love on you
It may seem hopeless
But fall on your knees
Give, your child, to Me
Master and Creator of all
The world, has it all wrong
The church, has gone wrong
I'm a Mighty Forceful Warrior
I can wipe out, the human race
Heal tragic disaster, in any place
I make things new, pure and true
I AM THAT I AM, Alpha and Omega
The First, Last, Beginning and the End
A Holy, All Powerful, yet, lowly Friend
I'm a loving Father, you can confide in!
A Father, who answers your prayers
A Father, who is near, right there
Right there, where you are
Mother, of a lost child
Let's converse a while. Give your, all to me! You will see
Your child's heart, is in My hand. I cause the weak to stand!
I confuse the wise. Ask me, for My eyes
So you can see, through Me
A powerful mystery
Hear Me speak
Listen for Me…

> *"Give all your worries and cares to God, for he cares about you."*
>
> *(1 Pet. 5:7)*

**I'm raising up Prophets. Pray for your child. Give him and her to me
I'm a mighty and powerful mystery. I hold you now, through eternity
Give it all right now, to Me!**

"The king's heart is a stream of water in the hand of the LORD;
he turns it wherever he will."
(Pro. 21:1)

"For I am about to do something new. See, I have already
begun! Do you not see it? I will make a pathway through the
wilderness. I will create rivers in the dry wasteland." (Is. 43:19)

"For I will pour water on the thirsty land, and streams on the
dry ground; I will pour my Spirit upon your offspring, and my
blessing on your descendants." (Is. 44:3)

"in the last days, God says, 'I will pour out my Spirit upon all
people. Your sons and daughters will prophesy. Your young men
will see visions, and your old men will dream dreams."
(Acts 2:17)

"I am Alpha and Omega, the First and the Last, the Beginning
and the End." (Rev. 22:13)

Prayer;

_____
_____
_____
_____
_____
_____
_____
_____
_____
_____
_____

Father – Mother - Grandparent

Listen; Father, mother, Grandparent, Auntie, Uncle
You, may NOT have done all you could have done
You possibly have done, the worse you could do
But Jesus, specializes in making all things new
He, takes what we sabotage, or mishandle
He renews, in His life and Holy Mantle
He takes our worse, and makes us live
Takes our ashes, and beauty He gives
Give, and it shall be given unto you
Watch Him make, it all brand new
When we have lost all our hope
He, gives His strength, to cope
To, regenerate a relationship
Pray His principles into place
And get in the Father's race
He that endures, to the end
Shall be saved, to live again
Continue to endure and pray
Jesus Christ, still the only way
Beauty for ashes. You are called
Holy, anointed, powerful, after all
The tears, the heartache, all the pain
He just takes it all, turns it toward gain
These are not just words. I know it's true
He takes all the bad, makes a miracle in you
It's not only true, because of the words I say
It's true, because of the results, when you pray
Father, Mother begin to pray. Satan's had his way
I am the One on the throne. In charge of everything
Hold your head up! Stop your sadness and your crying
Hold your head up! You are My child. Let's spend a while
Salvation is promised to your household. For, young and old
Get those names and begin to pray. Jesus Christ is the only way…

I have come to SEEK and SAVE those which are lost!

"Train up a child in the way he should go; even when he is old he will not depart from it." (Pro. 22:6)

"If we confess our sins, he is faithful and just and will forgive and purify us from all unrighteousness." (1 John 1:9)

"I acknowledge my sin to you, and I did not cover my iniquity...I will confess my transgressions to the LORD, and you forgave the iniquity of my sin..." (Ps. 32:5)

"People who conceal their sins will not prosper, but if they confess and turn from them, they will receive mercy." (Pro. 28:13)

"...Believe in the Lord Jesus and you will be saved, you and your household." (Acts 16:31)

"I am the way the truth and the life..." (John 14:6)

"...he will give a crown of beauty for ashes..." (Is. 61:3)

Prayer;

_____
_____
_____
_____
_____
_____
_____
_____
_____
_____
_____
_____

I Am the Righteousness of God

Seek First God **AND** His righteousness
I am HIs righteousness, the Son of God
I am Jesus Christ...Son of the living God!
Believe Me! I am bringing in My harvest
It's a lie, a sin, to believe anything false
It's a lie, to believe all prayer is lost
No, no, no! You are NOT defeated. No!
If drugs are involved, the answer is, No
If unhealthy relationship, the answer is, No
If, it's the low grades in class, must you ask
No matter your quest, Jesus Christ is BEST!
Recognize the issue. What is your problem?
Understand exactly what you're up against
Then, begin to stand holy and pray against
Submit to God, cast Satan out. He will flee
Out of your family, and your family tree
I cast out, every demon of fear and doubt. I cast out drugs. I cast out lust, fake love
I cast out spirits, not from God, above. I cast out rebellion. I cast out rejection
I cast out compulsive eating disorders. And I speak the greatest order, God's order
I cast down every deceptive and false imagination, that does not believe like Christ
I bring every thought, into the obedience of Christ. For you, I speak into existence
The perfect things of God. I speak into your life, all that's good, pure, full of love
Casting out fornication, sex without marriage. This, isn't God's living
This is improper, among God's creation. His children live pure and holy
You are loving sisters and brothers, until you get married to each other
So I cast down incest. Satan's offering to you, way less than God's best!
It is sin. All, sin brings death. Fornication, It's like a slow cooking, meth
Totally, eating up your insides. Devouring, all that's holy, all that's right
Flee sexual sin, this is your Father's word. I, Jesus Christ, must be heard
For you to live, any other teaching is a myth. Destroying your existence
I love you. I want to spend eternity with you. I have a great plan for you...

You know My teaching, of forgiveness and grace
Don't lose your way. Allow My grace to help you
Seek My face. Seek Me in all your ways
I Am the Way

"And this righteousness from God comes through faith in Jesus Christ to all who believe. There is no distinction: For all have sinned and fall short of the glory of God, and are justified freely by his grace through the redemption that is in Christ Jesus. God presented Him as an atoning sacrifice through faith in His blood, in order to demonstrate His righteousness, because in His forbearance, He had passed over the sins committed beforehand. He did this to demonstrate His righteousness at the present time, so as to be just and to justify the one who has faith in Jesus" (Rom. 3:22-26)

"Flee from sexual immorality…whoever sins sexually, sins against their own body." (Cor. 6:18)

"The wages of sin is death, but the gift of God is eternal life in Christ Jesus our Lord." (Rom. 6:23)

"We tear down arguments, and every presumption set up against the knowledge of God; and take captive every thought to make it obedient to Christ." (2 Cor. 10:5)

"…truly I say to you, whoever believes in me will also do the works that I do; and greater works than these will he do, because I am going to the Father." (John 14:12)

Prayer;

_____
_____
_____
_____
_____
_____
_____

Turn to Me

Parent of a lost child, it's been, a while
I've known you, before birth
I've known, every hurt
I've seen every tear
I've been right here
My word, must be read
This is the strength, you need
Learning My ways, helps you to see
It's not enough just to, 'think' you know Me
My word, is your answer! My Spirit will teach you!
You must believe. Be careful, the leader, you follow. It may be Satan's trick
If, the preacher's not coming into your neighborhood, their focus is a myth
It's very easy to know Me. Read the stories about Me. You, know I love hard
You know, I reach into the community and bring the lost to Me. You need Me
Not a counterfeit! Be careful of strange teachings, that make your soul uneasy
I am holiness! I am miraculous! I care for the lost! I 'seek out' the lost and hurt
This, is what you must find in a 'church'. A family of believers, seeking My ways
Going to the sinners, in the neighborhood and highways. Remember My ways!
I am love. I love all, everyone. I love all colors, all faces, all genders, all races
There is a problem, when a church facility, has all one color, unless none other
If, it's a country with mostly one race, well of course, this could be a good place
Now, if you live in the United States and only one race, mostly. Think carefully
Where the spirit of the Lord is, there is liberty, freedom. Freedom of racism
Freedom of fear. Freedom to go, and reach all souls near. I am the example
Don't let another, misrepresent Me. Your child needs the right way, taught
I, am the giver of life. You have been tried, tempted and bought! Live free!
Do not tangle back up with misery! Find a church of Liberty. Remember Me!
The poor, in the neighborhood should fit right in. I am a strong, drawing force
If, the poor are not coming in, simply pray and think again. Read, learn of Me
Start a non-profit and have bible study. Bring in prayer, love and study there
Do, what you read and leave the rest to Me. I am your hope, your salvation
I go and 'get' the lost. This is My word. This is My truth! I've come for you....

"Turn to me and be saved, all you ends of the earth; for I am God, and there is no other." (Is. 45:22)

Live My Word
And leave the rest to Me! I am with you always!

"I am here with you and will watch over you wherever you go...I will not leave you ..."(Gen. 28:15)

"...Believe in the Lord Jesus and you will be saved, you and your household." (Acts 16:31)

"He will bring you a message through which you and your household will be saved." (Acts 11:14)

"You rescue the humble...You light a lamp for me. The LORD, my God, lights up my darkness." (Ps. 18:27-28)

"Your word is a lamp to my feet and a light path." (Ps. 119:105)

"...The Holy Spirit ...will teach you all things and will remind you of everything I have said to you." (John 14:26)

"Make every effort to present yourself approved to God, an unashamed workman who accurately handles the word of truth." (2 Tim. 2:15)

"Now the Lord is the Spirit, and where the Spirit of the Lord is, there is freedom." (2 Cor. 3:17)

"...now is the time of God's favor, now is the day of salvation." (2 Cor. 6:2)

Prayer

_____
_____
_____
_____
_____
_____

Chapter Ten

POLICE OFFICER-
MY OBLIGATED BLUE

Praying for You

Police office I pray for you
We honor you
I need Angels to protect you
I need you
Now, I want to be clear
I love you, my love, my dear
Standing in the gap for your life
Lord take care of this husband or wife
Police officer, Thank you so, for your service
By now you know…
You don't need to be out there on that road
Without an understanding, of your destiny
You need to be free
But, don't only listen to me
Right now, you know that still, small voice
That's been telling you, to make this choice
This choice for Christ, and give your life
He gave His life, as your sacrifice
I need you, to make Him yours
He's knocking at your door
He's a great friend
You'll, have such comradery with Him
He knows all about your soul
Sees what you do, and where you go
Don't live this life and go without Him
The one and only, true best friend
He, places His Angels all around you
Officer, I need you. Stay safe, full of grace
Let Jesus go before you. And wisdom and mercy guide you
I need you. Jesus needs you. The city needs you
This world needs you…

> *"…I have called you friends, for all that I have heard from my Father I have made known to you."*
>
> *(John 15:15)*

God Bless you

"Ask and it will be given to you; seek and you will find; knock and the door will be opened to you." (Mat. 7:7)

"For he will command his angels concerning you to guard you in all you do."
(Ps. 91:11)

"The angel of the LORD encamps around those who fear him, and delivers them."
(Ps. 34:7)

"You are my friends if you do what I command."
(John 15:14)

Prayer;

_____
_____
_____
_____
_____
_____
_____
_____
_____
_____
_____
_____
_____

Choose You

Some, have made, wrong choices
But, you already deeply know this
Don't make the wrong, life choice
Cause, they may last forever
And they may go away, never
Please, accept My Father, in your life
He's the one, who makes, all things alright
He also, rights, all bad decisions, and wrong
He keeps you, faithful and keeps you strong
You need Him, in your life. He, is your living sacrifice
The world's not getting, too much better. We, need you, for the stormy weather
Thank you for your love, for your life, I know, it's so stressful at times
Especially when, you can't change or dictate to friends
They make their own decisions, ya' know
Just take Christ with you, wherever you go
I honor you. I really need you, in our city's life
Please, stand strong in your life
Stand, against wrong in your life
Jesus, keep you strong in your life
I, place God's blessings on your life
I, place blessings on your family tree
Jesus says, "I'm here, I need you for Me
To stand against evil with Me.
To keep My Children safe
Be careful, decisions you make
You, are in no position, to be fake
Meditate, My son My daughter, on My word
Pray My word. Keep the scriptures being heard
Faith comes by hearing. And hearing by My word
Increase your faith and daily pray. I need you this way
I have been your living sacrifice. Thank you for your life."

"Choose Me, I've already chosen you."
- Jesus

"It is the LORD who goes before you. He will be with you; he will not leave you or forsake you. Do not fear or be dismayed." (Deut. 3:18)

"Defend the weak and the fatherless; uphold the cause of the poor and the oppressed. Rescue the weak and the needy; deliver them from the hand of the wicked." (Ps. 82:3-4)

"My presence will go with you, and I will give you rest." (Ex. 33:14)

"...my power is made perfect in weakness..." (2 Cor. 12:9)

"...bad company corrupts good company." (1 Cor. 15:33)

"Don't repay evil for evil. Don't retaliate with insults when people insult you. Instead pay them back with a blessing. That is what God has called you to do, and he will bless you for it." (1 Pet. 3:9)

> *"Put on the whole armor of God, that you may be able to stand against the schemes of the devil."* (Eph. 6:11)

Prayer;

_____
_____
_____
_____
_____
_____

So Special you are

You've been very special to my family
One day you came, talked to my teen
I could tell, you were a believer too
You spoke like a big brother
Giving wisdom; I was so proud of you
Then, I saw you one day
You asked, had she found her way
I was so impressed with you. You know
Bad things are happening. No one can deny
It's, even in the church. Those among us
Causing hurt. Judas, betrayed Jesus
There are enemies, among us. So, surely among you
It can be expected. But like me, don't settle for it
Make your voice heard. Stand against wrong
In your own ranks
And I pray, that you're strong
I pray that your Families' live long
Your mom and dad, are so proud of you
And our Heavenly father, is smiling too
Know every day, we're praying for you
As you daily put on your badge
This is your medal of honor
Your shield of faith
Keep the faith
Talk to Jesus, He will talk back to you
He'll give you discernment, warnings too
Listen to, His still quiet or thunderous voice
In every choice, gently, loudly nudging you
Jesus, please take care of this man
This Officer and a gentleman
This Officer and a lady
We honor you…

"Fear of the LORD is the foundation of wisdom. Knowledge of the Holy One results in good judgement."

(Pro. 9:10)

So Special You Are!
Thank you, for your service!

"Commit you work to the Lord, and your plans will be established." (Pro. 16:3)

"Trust in the LORD with all your heart, and do not lean on your own understanding."
(Pro. 3:5)

"Bless those who curse you, pray for those who mistreat you."
(Luke 6:28)

"Then you will understand the fear of the LORD and find the knowledge of God." (Pro. 2:5)

"The Lord bless you and keep you; the Lord make his face shine on you and be gracious to you; the Lord turn his face toward you and give you peace." (Num. 6:24-26)

Prayer;

_____

_____

_____

_____

_____

_____

_____

_____

_____

_____

_____

_____

_____

Obligated Blue

You, are so beautiful to me
Beautiful, for my eyes to see
Evil lurking, searching all around
Jesus says, "On us, it won't be found."
Though, ten thousand fall at your feet
You will not be harmed, but protected
Though Satan shows his evil, ugly head
Tonight, you will be safe at home in your bed
Because, of you serving God and our country
Others, will live!
You serve the Lord!
Creator of the universe
You, serve the Lord!
My Obligated Blue…
An honorable name for you
Obligated to care and rescue
Obligated to be wise and strong
Obligated to stand against, wrong
Obligated to overcome evil with good
My, Obligated blue, I'm so proud of, you
So proud of your working toward
Hope for girls and boys
Police Officer
God bless you
God test you
You'll come out
As pure solid gold
Your story forever, told…

*"The name of the LORD is a strong tower; the righteous man runs into it and is **safe**."*

(Pro. 18:10)

Obligated blue…

I love you

"My victory and honor came from God alone. He is my refuge, a rock where no enemy can reach me." (Ps. 62:7)

"Though a thousand fall at your side, though ten thousands are dying around you, these evils will not touch you."

(Ps. 91:7)

"In the fear of the LORD one has strong confidence, and his children will have a refuge." (Pro. 14:26)

Prayer;

_____

_____

_____

_____

_____

_____

_____

_____

Home is Fine!

What's going on with family
You, cannot work under stress
Not, the worrying about fam kind
I, need you to know, all will be fine
Do the best, you can do, when at home
Rest and rejuvenate, don't stay up too late
Get your sleep. Healthy and organic, try to eat
Wish, my mom, could have made, you a meal
Now, that plate, was something, really real!
Yeah, you would have been truly convinced
Your plate, serious cookin' and immaculate!
She, never saved fine china, for another day
She said that day was special, because of you
I may have to make one of her dishes for you
Until then, we need to send some pizza your way
Listen when I tell you, you are loved beyond belief!
You are honored and adored, square up your shoulders
Put, that blue on with pride! Cause God is a living guide!
Today is a great day! You are being prayed for in true faith
You, take time to remind God, while reminding yourself
That today, dear Lord, I need Your help! I need You!
I recognize I am weak, but in You I am so strong
I take You with me today, as I drive **I watch and**

… PRAY

I pray for the city and all the families
I pray for city officials. I pray for me
I pray for my brothers and sisters
Beside me and in the community
I even pray for the 'real' church
To come out here, to the hurt
I use my words, my life Lord
To honor you…

"Watch and pray."

(Mat. 26:41)

My True Hero is You, Lord

"...may there be peace within your walls and prosperity in your palaces." (Ps. 122:7)

"You will keep in perfect peace all who trust in you, all whose thoughts are fixed on you." (Is. 26:3)

This is the day the Lord has made; let us rejoice and be glad in it." (Ps. 118:24)

"...God is our refuge and strength an ever-present help in trouble." (Ps. 46:1)

"Blessed are the peacemakers, for they shall be called the children of God." (Mat. 5:9)

"And those who are peacemakers will plant seeds of peace and reap a harvest of righteousness." (James 3:18)

Prayer;

_____
_____
_____
_____
_____
_____
_____
_____
_____
_____
_____

Chapter Eleven

CHURCH COME PRAY WITH ME

PRAYING ABOUT CRIME AND NOT GOING
OUT TO MAKE THEM MINE – IS DEAD FAITH

GO INTO THE HIGHWAYS AND I WILL TURN
THE LOST TO MY WAYS – JESUS   (1 COR. 3:6)

Church will you come, I'm lonely

Just an encouraging conversation or word
So much negative in my life, I've heard
I'd like to hear, that someone cares
And keeping me in their prayers
I ache so. I stay on the go
Satan, going to and fro
In my house, though
So much going on
I've grown use to it now
I need to climb out of this pit, somehow
Church, you hold the light to this world
Will you, shine it, in my little world
I'm sick, probably depressed
Yet, I don't even know it
You know, I just don't do, important things
Like, my appointments at the dentist
And ensuring, I have insurance
I'm just, living everyday
Just a cycle, this way
It would help, I know, if you came to pray
Others, I don't really know about
But me, I know about, me
When, you do, what
God says and, "Go"
It would help me, I know! Come to my house. Pray for me and all my children
Pray for me and my spouse. Pray for my kids, to live. Pray, we learn how to give
Give back to someone in need. Please help me, please. I can't speak for no one else
I can only speak for myself. I think, it's Jesus, I must need
Please, bring Him, to me...

> *"For where two or three gather in my name, there I am with them."*
>
> *(Mat.18:20)*

Please Come
Don't leave me out here to die all alone
Please Come!

"At one time we too were foolish, disobedient, deceived and enslaved by all kinds of passions and pleasures..." (Titus 3:3)

"...confess your sins to each other and pray for one another, that you may be healed. The prayer of a righteous person has great power as it is working." (James 5:16)

"...Satan answered the LORD and said, 'From going to and fro on the earth, and from walking up and down on it.'" (Job 1:7).

"The thief comes only to steal and kill and destroy. I have come that they may have life, and have it abundantly." (John 10:10)

"...they will lay hands on the sick, and they will be made well."
(Mark 16:18)

"Then the king said to the man of God, 'Intercede with the LORD your God and pray for me that my hand may be restored.' So the man of God interceded with the LORD, and the king's hand was restored and became as it was before."
(1 Kings 13:6)

"So after more fasting and prayer, the men laid their hands on them and sent them on their way." (Acts 13:3)

Prayer;

_____
_____
_____
_____
_____
_____
_____

I'm Just Like You

I'm an individual, just like you
Isn't, there any time, you need…
Do, you need, someone happy in your life
Do, you need, someone wise in your life
Do, you need, encouragement, in your life
Not someone, to always criticize, your life
That's what I need!
It would make me feel so good
To know, I've done good, with my family
And to know, Jesus has just been waiting on me
Teach me how, He knocks at my heart
Every second, waiting to start
A real relationship with me
How He longs to hold me, and direct me
Lead me out of this horrible place. Teach me to see His face
Teach me, there's more
More to this life than this. Oh, teach me, to bless
I know, I give off really bad vibes. I know I cheat. I know I lie
I know I'm stubborn and reluctant, too
I seem to have no desire, to grow out of this mess
But teach me anyway…to pray
To believe! Nothing's impossible for God
It's just, only impossible for me
But, if you pray with me
And I receive Him
Oh, what a victory, for me! I must have Him. I'm dying without Him
I'm slowly dying inside. I need REAL truth and a guide
I need His spirit in my life. Teach me how to hear
Teach me how, He is right here. So near
Calling me from, this fear
Calling my name…

My child, I'm right here

"...do not be grieved, for the joy of the LORD is your strength."
(Neh. 8:10)

"The LORD is near to the brokenhearted and saves those crushed in spirit." (Ps. 34:18)

"He heals the broken hearted and binds up their wounds."
(Ps. 147:3)

"Instruct those who are rich in the present age not to be conceited and not to put their hope in uncertainty of wealth, but in God, who richly provides all things for us to enjoy. Instruct them to do good, to be rich in good works, and to be generous and ready to share." (1 Tim. 6:18)

"Give and it will be given to you..." (Luke 6:38)

"I was hungry and you gave me something to eat, I was thirsty and you gave me something to drink, I was a stranger and you invited me in, I needed clothes and you clothed me, I was sick and you looked after me, I was in prison and you visited me.
(Mat. 25:35-36)

Prayer; **"With love and kindness have I drawn thee..."**

_____
_____
_____
_____
_____
_____
_____
_____
_____

Come and Get Me, so I Can, Go!

I live in a 'good' community
Most everyone, thinks I'm happy
But honestly, I've been wondering
Is there more to life, than these things
Don't get me wrong, I love my family
It just seems, something is missing
I tried. Nothing heals, my heart
Am I, missing something else
I have a lot of material stuff
And trust me, it's enough
Maybe, if the church
Would, come take me, to the hurt
It would bless me, to be a blessing
But, we only have a church service
Not involved in community service
I'm just unsettled, maybe nervous
I may find gifts, I didn't know I had
That's probably, just the lift I need
Giving away, a special part of me
It, could begin a cycle of giving
I think, this is what is missing
I just can't, put my finger on it
I need the church to come help
Shouldn't the pastor know this
Isn't this why, the church, exist
Making the world a better place
To, show the world, Jesus face
Doesn't the pastor know this
Doesn't he know, not going to the street, doesn't help the strong, to help the weak?
Doesn't he know, he can't just 'tell' everyone to, go. He or she has to, go also
He has to organize, and go do outreach. He has to lead, to effectively teach
He has to take us, to those in need. Jesus help us with, your ministry!
The church is the answer, to the street…

> "Now go! I will be with you as you speak, and I will instruct you in what to say."
>
> (Ex. 4:12)

> "Do not neglect your gift, which was given you in prophesy when the body of elders laid their hands on you."
> (1 Tim. 4:14)

My Gifts Are Well Kept Inside Me, So I Hurt Desperately
Please Come and Get Me!

"Go and announce to them that the kingdom of Heaven is near…Freely you have received, freely give." (Mat. 10:7-8)

"It is easier for a camel to pass through the eye of a needle than for a rich person to enter the kingdom of God." (Mark 10:25)

"Whoever trusts in his riches will fall, but the righteous will flourish like a green leaf." (Pro. 11:28)

"Carry each other's burdens, and in this way you will fulfill the law of Christ." (Gal. 6:2)

"To the weak I became weak, that I might win the weak. I have become all things to all people, that by all means I might save some." (1 Cor. 9:22)

"This will be your opportunity to serve as witnesses. So make up your mind not to worry beforehand how to defend yourselves. For I will give you speech and wisdom that none of your adversaries will be able to resist or contradict." (Luke 21:13-15)

"For at the time the Holy Spirit will teach you what you should say." (Luke 12:12)

"Whoever is generous to the poor lends to the LORD…"
(Pro. 19:17)

Prayer;

_____
_____
_____
_____
_____

Drug Addicts Live Near the Church

Girl 1 - Gurl, dat pasta' gettin' his money

Girl 2 - Girl, you crazy

Girl 1 - Honey, *and* he a, good man.
      He ain't even got, no udder, gurl
      He, take care his wife *and* his kids
      But, he ain't comin' out here, in dese streets
      Or going to the lost...Or, ta Sivadale or da County jail, cross downtown

Girl 2 - I thought they did, the block party and the bible school

Girl 1 - Gurl, day do dat, fo dos peoples

Girl 2 - What?

Girl 1- What day gonna' tell da peoples? Specially, day a franchise

Girl 2 - A franchise. What, is you talkin' about?

Girl 1 - Okay. Da peoples got to know, day, doin' outreach, fo da donations
     So, day have da block party, two times fo da year and do Vacation
     Bible School, FO DAYS, fo da year, sometimes three days
     And day take, little bit of food cans, down to da soup kitchen, cross town
     Now, dats, what day do!

Girl 2 - So, you tellin' me. The 'good' pastors, now, are just like the 'bad' pastors

Girl 1 - Nowwww...you got it!

Girl 2 - Well, why do you think that is?

Girl 1 - Gurl...Do da crack head, come out da house and day got da crack?
     No!
     Do, da deer come out, to da pasture and she got da food, in da woods?
     No!
     Do, da fish come out da water? Do da snail, leave his shell?
     What, I'm tellin' you is, da paastas got every thang, day need!
     Honey, this whole city can go ta hell, long as day livin' well
     And, you don't think it's true
     Let dese folk, start killin' one another, and see, if day come fo you!
     Gurl, day is on, da udder side of town, at home, feet up, large screen on
     Food, on da TV tray, ain't comin' back till' Wednesday
     Honey, Church doors ain't even open, if you want to ask somebody to pray

Girl 2 – Mmm Mmm Mmm...Lord have Mercy, have Mercy!

Will the Pastors, go and set the captives free, in the neighborhoods?
Teach the sheep to Win the Lost. This was Jesus' Ministry
"I came to SEEK and to SAVE the lost." -Jesus

"...you will receive power when the Holy Spirit comes on you; and you will be my witnesses for Me, both in Jeruselem and in all Judea and Samaria, and to the ends of the earth."
(Acts 1:8)

"...Defend the oppressed..." (Is. 1:17)

"Go rather to the lost sheep....As you go, preach this message: '-The kingdom of heaven is near.' Heal the sick, raise the dead, cleanse the lepers, drive out demons. Freely you have received; freely give..." (Mat. 10:6-7)

"Each of you should look not only look to your own interest, but also to the interest of others." (Phil. 2:4)

"...In the last days, terrible times will come. For men will be lovers of themselves, lovers of money... lovers of pleasure rather than lovers of God...having a form of godliness but denying it's power. Turn away from such as these!" (2 Tim. 3:1-5)

"...In my name they will drive out demons..." (Mat. 17:17)

"For the Son came to SEEK and to SAVE the lost." (Luke 19:10)

"...Go, into the highways...and compel people to come..."
(Luke 14:23)

Prayer;

_____

_____

_____

_____

_____

Who will Come for Me?

Come, get me please
If, you don't come get me
Who, will come and find me
Will, you let Satan, take me, out
With hopelessness, fear and doubt?
Will, you help me change my destiny?
Right now, I'm headed to destruction
With no wise counsel and instruction
My family, they try to meet my needs
But, life has become, too much for me
It seems like, life is working against me
I don't know, I'm working against myself
I'm gonna' die out here, without your help
I really need God. I need the REAL Church
That's the only power, that's gonna' work
I'm a captive, that must clearly be, set free
I'm held captive, inside of me

The church is searching

To find, their purpose …I know their purpose. Their purpose is me

I'm lost, so very lost. So deep in the valley, so far in the woods
I can't even recognize, good. You'll have to pray for me
You may even have to spend a little time with me

You, may have to bring some things, I need

You may have to bring, everything I need
Most all I need, is covered under love
Everything I need, is from above
Introduce me, to my provider
My knight in shiny armor

My friend, that sticks closer than a brother. Teach me to read and study
Teach me how to live, happily. Happy is he, who's God, is the Lord…

> *"…With
> unfailing love
> **I have drawn
> you***
> *to myself."*
>
> *(Jere. 31:3)*

> *"…there is a friend
> who sticks closer
> than a brother."*
> *(Pro.18:24)*

Happy I'll be, if you show Him, to me!
Thank you, Lord

"They preached the gospel in that city and made many disciples." (Acts 14:21)

"...Joyful indeed are those whose God is the Lord." (Ps. 144:15)

"...all sinners will be destroyed; there will be no future for the wicked." (Psalm 37:38)

"Friends, why are you doing this? We too are only human, like you. We are bringing you good news, telling you to turn from these worthless things to the living God, who made the heavens and the earth and the sea and everything in them." (Acts 14:15)

"Once we, too, were foolish and disobedient. We were misled and became slaves to many lusts and pleasures. Our lives were full of evil and envy, and we hated each other." (Titus 3:3)

"Satan comes to steal, kill and destroy..." (John 10:10)

"Go and make disciples..." (Mat. 28:19)

"A friend loves at all times and a brother is born for adversity." (Pro. 17:17)

Prayer;

_____

_____

_____

_____

_____

_____

_____

Chapter Twelve

G.A.N.G. – GOD'S ANOINTED NEED GOD

Consider This - God's Anointed Need God

Because of decisions, and the way you live
Takin' lives, my forgiving Father, gives
I wanted to tell you somethin'
You gettin' whipped. Satan, got you tricked!
I'm praying in the night. In prayer for your fight
God keeps showing me, how much He loves you
How you've lost your, way. How, you have gone astray
He has shown me, your hurt. Others, treated you, like dirt
Telling you, you are nothing. Even, showing you, the same
Strategized, you livin' all together. Satan, the author of this game
He created this maze, with your life, but Jesus came, to give you life
Don't make choices that go the wrong way. Let's get together and pray
Put, new businesses in our hood. Use the profit, like we should
Helping one another, and others. Taking back, your brothers
You got to use your mind. Stop wasting your time
Everyone, in the neighborhood, pray and raise '
Hard work and money, to build that hood
Turn it powerfully around for the good!
Meet together. **Find a 'real' leader, sold out to Christ!**
Give your offering and tithes. Watch how you ARISE!
Those church buildings in your hood
Got their doors locked all week!
A hireling and his sheep
You better wake up!
You sleep!

Your Answer is with a REAL Leader of Christ
Connect with a 'real' leader, who earnestly serves Christ
This will turn the
ENTIRE
HOOD'S LIFE!
You will know by their fruit to save the lost
To build the community, the elderly, the youth
Any other way, is Not the truth

"The eyes of the LORD are on the righteous, and his ears attentive to their cry." (Ps. 34:15)

"The LORD hears his people when they call to him for help. He rescues them from all their troubles." (Ps. 34:17)

"He fulfills the desires of those who fear him; he hears their cries for help and rescues them." (Ps.145:19)

"Our ancestors were unfaithful and did what was evil in the sight of the LORD our God. They abandoned the LORD and his dwelling place; they turned their backs to him." (2 Chron. 29:6)

"We know that God does not listen to sinners, but He does listen to the one who worships Him and does His will." (John 9:31)

"listen to my prayer! Look down and see me praying night and day for your people...I confess that we have sinned against you. Yes, even my own family and I have sinned." (Neh. 1:6)

"Oh Lord, hear my voice! Let your ears be attentive to the voice of my pleas..." (Ps. 130:2)

Angela - "Heavenly Messenger"

Prayer

_____

_____

_____

_____

_____

_____

_____

_____

Think and Rethink - Gods Anointed Need God –

Wake up, Oh sleeper. The leaders teachin', changin' their preachin'
Their message has no power! No real power. Sounds smooth
But, you need, the power of a mighty God's hand
You, think you aren't your brother's keeper?
Picking and choosin', who to protect
What, a tangled web 'we've', net
Satan's plan is to destroy you
He has preachin' wolves, in on it too
You're tricked by liars - wolves, hirelings
They're your real enemies, all laughin' at you
'They' shakin' their head at the crime you do
And you too, should be ashamed of you
Are you savaged, uneducated, beasts?
I suggest you listen to My Daddy!
Education, yes all should get it
Will help you, in this life, to live it
But you gettin' tricked by all those myths
JESUS CHRIST IS THE ANSWER, to all of this!
I'm so tired of you treatin' My Daddy like a punk
You think 'cause 'they' got houses and cars, they the junk
They, are the, true punks! That's not the answer, to survival!
Don't you ever read your bible! My Father can change your life in a second
If you don't believe that, get to steppin'. He, will put a blessing on you
That will give you power, in all you do! Education, it's God's way
Will improve your life, all you do and say. All, should get it
But, 'the total answer' to this life you livin'
Is still God's Son. The only answer
The only answer that's real, is
The only answer still…

The WAY, the TRUTH and the LIFE!
The Only Answer is JESUS CHRIST!

I'm tired of fake lives
I pray you choose the real life!
- The Fire of Jesus Christ – Angela

"...the word of God is alive and powerful..." (Heb. 4:12)

"Don't copy the behavior and customs of this world, but let God transform you into a new person by changing the way you think. Then you will learn to know God's will for you..."
(Rom. 12:2)

"Anyone born of God refuses to practice sin, because God seed abides in him; he cannot go on sinning, because he has been born of God." (1 John 3:9)

"For you have been born again, but not to a life that will quickly end. Your new life will last forever because it comes from the eternal, living word of God." (1 Pet. 1:23)

"...Now that you have escaped the corruption in the world caused by evil desires...make every effort to add to your faith virtue; add to virtue knowledge; add to knowledge, self-control, perseverance; and to perseverance, godliness; and to godliness, brotherly kindness; and to brotherly kindness, love. For if you possess these qualities and continue to grow in them, they will keep you from being ineffective and unproductive in your knowledge of our Lord Jesus Christ."
(2 Pet. 4-8)

Prayer;   **"Let brotherly love continue." (Heb. 13:1)**

_____

_____

_____

_____

_____

_____

Earnest Prayer - Gods Anointed Need God!

Jesus, bless these special ones on gangs! Show them the power in your name
I send up this earnest prayer, commanding the atmosphere. Pray with me
Whatever I bind on earth, is bound in heaven. - - Jesus in your name
I bind up and cast out theses spirits of lust, death and destruction
I cast out the spirit of abuse, neglect, anger and rejection
And I replace it with a heart of forgiveness and affection
To live, an amazing life. I cast out the spirit of pride
Heal, Lord, this young, this old, deep hurt inside
I, cast out anger, envy, jealousy, lust, addiction
These evil spirits have no power, in this city
Even though, society here, has failed them
And the 'church folk 'not coming for them
Use us Lord, for your perfect glory, Lord
Jesus wake these young, up at night
Give them a vision of what's right
This prayer is reaching there. Faith, without works is going nowhere
Jesus, send your *real* church, to do your powerful, *real* work.
The saints are stayin' in, 'confused' about your word
Because, the truth is not being heard. Preachers
Preachin' for their personal success and gain
Hirelings, causing the world to stay the same
If my people which are called by my name
Would humble themselves and pray. Turn from wicked ways
I'll heal the land, forgive their sins and better the days
Jesus is exposing the evilness, in their ways
Revealing, the truth in their lives and lies. Lord, give the, true Church Your eyes
Your wisdom. Your understanding. Your heart, to reach the lost
Not, to pick and choose. For, any sinner will do…

**God chooses the gang member, the lost, the homeless, the hurting
The poor, the desperate, heartbroken rich, the elderly, the prisoner, the sick.
They're all on God's, hurting heart's list**

Dear Jesus, place on fire for You, the one reading this

"...Truly I say to you, the tax collectors and the prostitutes go into the kingdom of God before you." (Mat. 31:31)

"Whatever you bind on earth is bound in heaven, and whatever you loose on earth will be loosed in heaven." (Mat. 18:18)

"Gracious words are like a honeycomb, a sweetness to the soul and health to the body." (Pro. 16:24)

"...to bestow on them beauty for ashes..." (Is. 61:3)

"And the LORD listened to Hezekiah's prayer and healed the people." (2 Chron. 30:20)

"If My people which are called by my name..." (2 Chron. 7:14)

*"**Praise the LORD**, my soul, and forget not all his benefits— who forgives all your sins and heals all your diseases, who **redeems your life** from the pit and crowns you with love and compassion, who satisfies your desires **with good things** so that your youth is renewed like an eagle's. The LORD works righteousness and justice for all the oppressed."*
(Psalm 103:6)

Prayer;

_____

_____

_____

_____

_____

_____

_____

_____

From Heaven: Honor & Respect is Best

I have to converse with you
Tell you what, My Father says
Hear, no lies! We must tell the truth
The friends up here, trying to warn you
We need you. The world needs you…to change
Everyone needs to see, you are no longer the same
The neighborhood, is totally lost. They need hope again
I speak to you from Heaven, my friend. It's outrageous, beautiful
In here. I have no loss. I have no fear. Just not ready, for you here
I'm pleading, for the love we share. Pleading for our memories there
Don't leave me out, of anywhere. Have a cookout! Laugh with me
I'm singing now. I'm truly free. Man, this is your homie, it's me
No more, fighting please. Do this for me. No drugs. Just hugs
Keep it real. You know I'm right. I gotta' claim your sight
I need, to get you to see. You got to live free, with me
Put down the guns. Leave the drugs. Man you smart
I always knew, you were so talented. It was you
Makin' music. Makin' raps. Spreadin' laughs
It was you! I need you! I believe in you!
Stay on earth, a while. Show your real style. Smartest on earth, your birth
You've been tricked. Lied to and deceived. Drank from the wrong fountain
You my friend, reach high. The tallest mountain. The sky. The absolute best
Get help, with your dreams. Do it for you. Do it for me. Do it for, the family!
Stay there. My best advice, is to help the young, to live again, to respect again
No Sir, Yes Maam, let's start that, again. Nothing is wrong, in showing honor
Everything's right about it. Jesus did it. While we were sinners, He died for us
When we do wrong, He still yet, longs for us. Shines the sun and the moon on us
You know, we don't deserve it, but He does it anyway. That's His, kind of way
Bring honor back to the hood. Do as we should. Give your lives to Jesus Christ
This will bring honor to God. Living His word. Sharing His word. Living His way
Trust and pray. Let Him turn your life around. Do this somehow, for me right now!

Dear Lord, teach me honor, and all that's good
You're the greatest example, for my hood
- Love, your friend from heaven

"Don't let anyone think less of you because you are young. But set an example to all believers in what you say, in the way you live, in your love, your faith, and your purity." (1 Tim. 4:12)

"Defend the weak and fatherless..."
(Ps. 82:3)

"May he defend the afflicted among the people and save the children of the needy; may he crush the oppressor."
(Ps. 72:4)

"For he stands at the right hand of the needy one, to save him from those who condemn his soul to death."
(Ps. 109:31)

Prayer;

_____
_____
_____
_____
_____
_____
_____
_____
_____
_____
_____
_____
_____
_____
_____
_____
_____
_____

Don't Come Here...Friend

I'm burnin' in here
I can't concentrate
I didn't wanna' come here
I want my chance, for Heaven
Now this sister, is writin' this book
Late at night, she cryin', for my soul
I'm burnin' on fire! I didn't wanna go
She's cryin' so! God said, I could let you know
How much pain I'm in, and how it's never gonna end
She's writing for me, so you won't come in here, with me
Please! Stop killin', my friend. I don't want you to end, in here
Go to heaven, so I can think about you, near
Give your life to Christ, so I can know
There is still some good, that I sow
You know this is from me, cause' you know me
You know, what I think and what I was truly like
And you know I wouldn't want you here
Please honor me! Give your life to Christ
I, plead with you, straight from hell. I'm telling you, man, start over new
Homie, I'll be so very proud of you. And I got to tell you, somethin' else
I need you man! You gotta' help
Help everyone, not to come in here
If a river could cry, it would be the tears from my eyes
I hurt my family and my friends, you know my mama, cryin'
I can't see, and laugh, and love and walk and talk again
So I need you, to live for you, live for me. I need a legacy
Put my name on some shirts. And vow to never, ever hurt
Go see my family. Tell my mama for me
You're gonna' live your life free. Grant my request...honor me

Honor me, with your life, please honor me
You know me... BFF
- Best Friends Forever -

> *"Repent,*
>   *for the*
> *kingdom of*
> *heaven has*
> *come near."*
>
> *(Mat. 3:2)*

"And he will answer, 'I tell you, I do not know where you are from. Depart from me, all you evildoers.' There will be weeping and gnashing of teeth when you see Abraham, Isaac, Jacob, and all the prophets in the kingdom of God, but you yourselves are thrown out."
(Luke 13:27-28)

Prayer;

_____

_____

_____

_____

_____

_____

_____

_____

_____

_____

_____

_____

_____

_____

_____

_____

_____

_____

_____

_____

_____

_____

Chapter Thirteen

MY PRAYER

JESUS I TRUST YOU
I TRUST - ONLY YOU.

Present my Body a Living Sacrifice

Jesus, You, heal all wounds, all pain
Take this heart, and make me, again
I need to act like, I know, who I am
Apart, from my past pain and friends
Lord, who do you, need me to be
That is who, my heart longs to be
I've sinned in situations, I've been in
I've sinned with evil thoughts, I held in
I've sinned, tempted with temptation
Placing myself, in places I should not
Choosing not, to do things, I ought
Sin sets in, when I don't give in, to you
You must have, every fiber, every desire
My thoughts, My actions, every part of me
Please forgive me. I give all of me, to you
Please forgive me, Lord, and make me new
Whatever situation I am in, I praise you!
Each day, I awake, to give all glory to you
This is perfect praise, when I wholly praise you

"This means anyone who belongs to Christ has become a new person.
The old life is gone;
a new life has begun.

(2 Cor. 5:17)

I don't wait, for the perfect job, house or car. Those are not, where my praises are
Satan, what a liar you are! JESUS CHRIST, I submit my life, a living sacrifice
To You. Right where I am, is a perfect place, to praise you. It's perfect praise
When things, aren't 'my' way. Cause Father, you make my day, perfect
You make days, perfect. You make my way, straight
When all glory goes to you, it's perfect praise!
In the hard places, I give you perfect praise
Father, where I am, at this moment
 I give you perfect praise…
You deserve every
Part of me…
TOTALLY!

I give my all, to you. That's the perfect thing, I'll do
 Thank you, for loving me, and all that you do!

Father, I love you

"At this, Job got up tore his robe and shaved his head. Then he fell to the ground in worship and said, 'Naked I came into my mother's womb, and naked I will depart. The LORD gave and the LORD has taken away; may the name of the LORD be praised'" (Job 1:20-21)

"He restores my soul. He leads me in paths of righteousness for his name's sake." (Ps. 23:3)

"...You, LORD, are our Father. We are the clay you are the potter; we are all the work of your hand." (Is. 64:8)

"God did this so that they would seek him and perhaps reach out for him and find him, though he is not far from any of us. For in him we live and move and have our being... We are his offspring." (Acts 17:27-28)

"'For I know the plans I have for you,' declares the Lord, 'plans to prosper you and not to harm you, plans to give you hope and a future.'" (Jere. 29:11)

Kanisa
- The Church

Prayer

_____

_____

_____

_____

_____

_____

_____

_____

_____

_____

A Living Sacrifice Died, for Me

Whatever moment this is, it's yours Father
Whatever's bad or good, you're in control
You are my head. I give you, complete control
I ask you, to place me, where you want me
Put desires in my heart, where you need me
Don't let me fall, into this sinful, worldly pit
And praise you only, because of 'things' I get
Don't let me live, 'in forget'…
Forgetting your heart
Forgetting to keep, my life and sin apart
Forgetting to reach out, with your word
Forgetting to be bold and speak, all I've heard
Anything, short of your word, I can't do
NOTHING, satisfies me, but all of you
I can't have a form of you, denying your power
I've got to have all of you and all of your power
I've got to pray, every hour, all of the day
I've got to pray, every sinner makes their way
Into your Kingdom, for this is your whole heart
Reuniting with your children, no longer apart
So Father, I pray right now, that you send workers
Laborers of love, just like you, into your harvest
Out of your Holy Kingdom, send laborers, Lord
Laborers, Into the highways and hedges
With your delivering and powerful message

You, gave us clear instructions to, 'Go'…

Let us arise now, from among the goats

> *"He is the atoning sacrifice for our sins, and not only for ours but for the sins of the whole world."*
>
> *(1 John 2:2)*

"This is love: not that we loved God, but that he loved us and sent his Son as an atoning sacrifice for our sins."
(1 John 4:10)

"...God demonstrates his own love for us in this: While we were still sinners, Christ died for us." (Rom. 5:8)

"The harvest is plentiful, but the workers are few.
Ask the Lord of the harvest, therefore to send out workers into His harvest field." (Luke 10:2)

"He who did not spare his own Son, but gave him up for us all--how will he not also, along with him,
graciously give us all things." *(Rom. 8:32)*

"For God so loved the world that he gave his one and only Son, that whoever believes in him shall not perish but have eternal life. For God did not send his Son to condemn the world, but to save the world through Him."
(John 3:16-17)

Prayer

_____

_____

_____

_____

_____

_____

_____

_____

_____

I Need Spiritual Eyes

Father, I got to have your back
Satan's coming full force, with his attack
We're sittin' back! I can't sit back
It's so clear to me, now
We've gotten far off path, somehow
It's because of the messengers, Lord
Jesus, send your true messengers, Lord
It always baffles me. These fakes
Don't go, to set captives free
I tell you, that baffles me
Our Father wants sinners, set free
But, now Lord, I clearly see
Remove these scales, from our eyes
That we may all see, clearly
Confusion, You're not the author of
So Lord, make clear, Your true love
Show us, what a true sheep looks like
So we don't get distracted, in this fight
We're following fake leaders…
Wolves, dogs, goats, false teachers
Because, of their ways, we do not, 'Go'
They teach us what, we **do not** know!... we do not, 'Go'
We need real shepherds, for your flocks. Jesus, we're ready!
Show us what you got! Your word says, we're just like You, Lord
When Elisha's servant looked up and opened his eyes. He saw, there were more
With us, then against us. Lord I plead, lead us to your true Shepherds. Show us
Through spiritual eyes, to win the lost, at any cost. Not just a slogan, but for real
Lord, let us talk to no one, that down plays, this burden that we feel**…**

> *"Not everyone who says to me, 'Lord, Lord,' will enter the kingdom, but only the one who does the will of my Father who is in heaven."*
> *(Mat. 7:21)*

> *"Do not merely listen to the word, and so deceive yourselves. Do what it says."*
> *(James 1:22)*

Jesus, You're my 'real!'

"No one knows the thoughts of God except the Spirit of God. What we have received is not the spirit of the world, but the spirit who is from God, so we may understand what God has freely given us." (1 Cor. 2:11-12)

"When the servant of the man of God got up early the next morning and went outside, there were troops, horses, and chariots everywhere. 'Oh, sir, what will we do now?' the young man cried to Elisha. 'Don't be afraid!' Elisha told him. "For there are more on our side than on theirs!' Then Elisha prayed, 'Oh Lord, open his eyes and let him see!' The Lord opened the Young man's eyes, and when he looked up, he saw that the hillside around Elisha was filled with horses and chariots of fire." (2 Kings 6:15-16)

"Go into the highways and byways and compel others to come..." (Luke 14:23)

"Why do you call me 'Lord, Lord,' and do not do what I say?" (Luke 6:46)

Prayer;

_____

_____

_____

_____

_____

_____

_____

_____

_____

Not Distracted Anymore

Close that door! Not distracted anymore
Following "church", is what I followed, Lord
You never said, follow church, but you, Lord!
You always teach your sheep, to follow you
Even, consistently and clearly warning us
"BEWARE" …WOLVES ARE EVERYWHERE!
Never, ever take your eyes off Jesus, Angie
She, made sure to tell me. Thank you! Ruby
She said, Keep your eyes on Jesus Christ. She, was a "church going" girl back then
However, I had just given my life, to Him. She knew, I may lose my way, someday
Following leaders. Not following His way. I must tell you, my Sis, I came to my end
"Church" almost killed me. Do you feel me? Following fake leaders, false prophets
And goats. Serving under wolves, will kill you, ya' know. Lord help me to never
Give myself, to a ministry, that the word of God, is not lived, with integrity
When Christ Jesus, is *truly* your teacher, you know what to look for, exactly
The fruit of the Spirit or lack of, is evident. We should clearly see
The fruit of our work. We are instructed to win the lost, and the hurt
Yes, we are saved, only by grace! Yet, Christ says, we are saved unto
His mighty, work! What fruit do we display, to show the world, His way?
Leaders are seeking, the "churched". We're looking around, at one another
In the pews. The world is looking back at us, baffled too
Why, is the local church, not reaching, the prisoner?
Or the addict, the homeless, the hungry, in their city?
The empty, the hurt, the jobless, the gangs, the prostitute
I refuse to only, sit in pews. Lead me Lord, to fulfill ministry
With goals just like you. Help me to reach, the hurt souls for you…

**My spirit to discern. My hands to heal. My heart to feel. My legs to walk
My words to talk. Jesus get my brothers and sisters out of the pews
You have a mighty work, for us to do!**

**"Go into the highways and byways…" -Jesus
(Luke 14:23)**

"I am sending you out like sheep among wolves..." (Mat. 10:16)

"...Come follow me, and I will show you how to fish for people."
(Mat. 4:19)

"So the word of God spread. The number of disciples in
Jerusalem increased rapidly, and a large number of priests
became obedient to the faith." Now Stephen, a man full of God's
grace and power, performed great wonders and signs among
the people. (Acts 6:7)

"in this way the word of the Lord spread and grew in power."
(Acts. 19:20)

"If anyone wants to be my follower, **you must turn from your**
selfish ways*, take up your cross and follow me."*
(Mat. 16:24)

"Very truly I tell you, whoever believes in me will do the works
I have been doing, and they will do even greater things
than these..." (John 14:12)

Prayer;

_____

_____

_____

_____

_____

_____

_____

_____

_____

_____

I'm with You Lord

Jesus…

I must give perfect praise to You

I can't live less, than You desire

And I can't live, without Your heart fire

Where is, what You gave, Jeremiah, Lord; Where's that righteous, burning fire, Lord

Messages now, so clear about prosperity; You came, that we might live, abundantly

The preachers, are surely preaching this; In the last days, we'll be lovers of ourselves

So trust me, they've got, everyone seeking "HELP". I'm just asking. Where is **Your**

Righteous fire, Lord. See, when my child is dying, I need Your fire, Lord

When, my heart is breaking, I need Your fire, Lord. When, the lost are bound

I need Your fire, Lord; When, I'm losing my way, I need Your fire, Lord

When, I'm making decisions, I need Your fire, Lord

I have to remember Your heart's desires, Lord

I need Your wisdom, to think like You. I need a holy, bold fire and desire, Lord

To reach like You. Wisdom in the local church, is not really, clearly recognized

But, **I'm with you, Lord.** I know, He that wins souls is wise

We are looking, pondering in…Surprise! We have truly forgotten

To win others to Christ. And to present our bodies, a living sacrifice

Jesus use my gifts. Lord, I give them to you. To spread your word

Is my only "true". I got to live like you! All you ever wanted to do

Is live, what your Father in Heaven, wanted you to

And You taught us, to be just like You!

To live like You. Teach like You

Reach like You. Heal like You

Cast out evil spirits, like You

And none of this is any good

Unless we love, just like You

With Your ways, every day!

Jesus, I bind these wolves

In Jesus name, they're fake

Their message, will fall on deaf ears

Jesus Christ, commands the atmosphere!

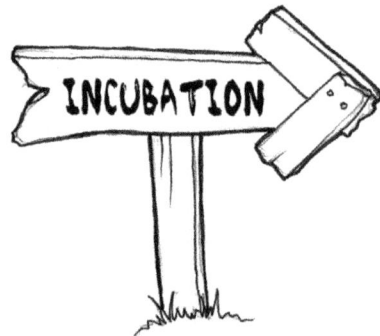

Jesus, Win The Local Church, Back to You! These Hirelings, Are Threw!

JESUS, WE SERVE THE LOST…WITH ACTION!

"But if I say I'll never mention the LORD or speak his name, his word burns in my heart like a fire. It's like a fire in my bones! I am worn out trying to hold it in! I can't do it!"
(Jere. 20:9)

"Pray also for me, that whenever I speak, words may be given me so that I will fearlessly make known the mystery of the gospel, for which I am an ambassador in chains. Pray that I declare it fearlessly, as I should." (Eph. 6:19-20)

"Therefore, since we have such hope, we are very bold."
(2 Cor. 3:12)

"Can any one of you by worrying add a single hour to your life. And why do you worry about clothes? See how the flowers of the field grow. They do not labor or spin. Yet I tell you that not even Solomon in all his splendor was dressed like one of these. If that is how God clothes the grass of the field, which is here today and tomorrow is thrown into the fire, will he not much more clothe you- you of little faith?" (Mat. 27-30)

"...And whoever captures souls is wise." (Pro. 11:30)

Prayer;

_____
_____
_____
_____
_____
_____
_____
_____
_____

Dear Jesus I'm Here

I've got to be filled, with your spirit
Always giving thanks, in your spirit
No speaking, untrue or carnal things
Only speaking your word, my King
Got to get close, to your holiness
I got to preach it, with boldness
You say, "Be holy, for I am holy"
You're a Pure, Holy Miracle to me
A Holy God, loving and kind to me
You are the ANSWER, to all things
The way, the truth, the life, my King
In all that I do, I must represent You
You are mine! You got all, my time!
I'm forever Yours! I won't be lured!
Separated from You once, by sin
I got to get close to You, again
You have forgiven me, set me free
Don't let me fall, into what I see
I need spiritual eyes. I need Thee
You say, we will know one another
Yet, we're calling wolves, our brother
You've taught us, to look at the fruit; Even if a man, appears to be good
Preaching and teaching your word. Has been changed, by what he's heard
Sinners, held captive, must be free; We're still playing and living casually
People are living, dying and going to hell! Where's the sense of urgency
Among Your children, to tell?
Meeting among, ourselves
Will not stop, those held captive
The prostitute, the addicted, the lost, from going to hell…

Let's Set Captives Free. Let's Pray. Let's Plan
Let's Organize. Jesus Says, Winning Souls Is Wise!
Dear Jesus, Give The Church Your Eyes!

"Yet I have this against you: You have forsaken the love you had at first." (Rev. 2:4)

"Because of the increase of wickedness, the love of most will grow cold, but the one who stands firm to the end will be saved." (Mat. 24:12-13)

"...In the last time there would be scoffers whose purpose in life is to satisfy their ungodly desires. These people are the ones who are creating divisions among you. They follow their natural instincts because they do not have God's Spirit in them." (Jude 1:18-19)

"...My righteous one SHALL LIVE BY FAITH, and if he shrinks back, my soul has no pleasure in him. But we do not belong to those who shrink back and are destroyed, but to those who have faith and are saved." (Heb. 10:38-39)

"Sanctify them by the truth; your word is truth; as you have sent me into the world. I have sent them into the world." (John 17:17-18)

"...He that winneth souls is wise."

(Pro. 11:30)

Prayer;

_____
_____
_____
_____
_____
_____
_____

I Forgive you

Jesus…
I give, my entire self to You
My many imperfections too
All I've been through
Everyone in my life
Past or present
I've forgiven
Can't let nothin'
Hinder my livin'
Finally, I know
Struggles and trials
Make us, who we are
We can't judge from afar
We must be, up and close
So, if you acted like an animal
Devouring or destroying my soul
It wasn't what you wanted, to do
It's the enemy, who controlled you
If you neglected me, with your greed
Not including me, losing your blessing
It's okay. My Father, kept me anyway
If you hurt me, because of trickery and lies
Daddy has now, given me, His perfect eyes
I see clearer now. Before, I was lost somehow
If you hurt me, because you just wanted to abuse me
I forgive you. I forget you. It wasn't you. I know it was the enemy
Who, seeks to destroy me. Now, the Lord has made me strong
I will deliver the oppressed! Lord, thank you for my test
God bless and forgive you. I've been to life's school
The enemy is my footstool. Lord, forgive me
For the times, I caused others harm be...
Forgive me, for when I sinned
I've done terribly wrong
Thank you, dear Lord
Now I'm strong
I forgive, my
Enemies…

I Forgive you. May God please, Bless you!
Amen

"For you know that when your faith is tested, your endurance has a chance to grow. So let it grow, for when your endurance is fully developed, you will be perfect and complete and needing nothing." (James 1:3-4)

"So we have stopped evaluating others from a human point of view..." (2 Cor. 5:6)

"Put on all of God's armor so that you will be able to stand firm against all strategies of the devil. For we are not fighting against flesh-and-blood enemies, but against evil rulers and authorities of the unseen world, against mighty powers in this dark world, and against evil spirits in heavenly places." (Eph. 6:11-12)

"Get rid of all bitterness, rage, harsh words, and slander, as well as all types of evil behavior. Instead be kind to each other, tenderhearted, forgiving one another, just as God through Christ has forgiven you." (Eph. 4:31-32)

"And forgive us our sins, as we have forgiven those who sin against us." (Mat. 6:12)

Tisha
-Anointed

Prayer to forgive;   - Forgiveness - It must be...

_____
_____
_____
_____
_____
_____
_____
_____

No Other God

In giving you perfect praise
Father, it's You, who is perfect
I never feel less, than anyone
In size, height, shape or form
I'm thinking, only about Jesus
No one has a say, in my destiny
If, you choose to invest in me
It will bless me and bless you
Your choice, won't stop me
Whatever, you decide to do
It is between, God and you
Thank you! God bless you!
I got my eyes, on the prize
My greatest Life Prize…MY
Father's eyes. JESUS CHRIST
My heart's focus, on the lamb
  - **I AM THAT I AM.**
Got my mind, on things above
Praying and fasting, in His love
Cause, it's all about You, Jesus
I'll never take Your praise away
Cause Father, it's all about You
Each and every day. Your ways
How I need You. How I want You
How I adore You. Bow before You
How I cherish You. Talk with You
Laugh with You. Totally trust You
I Live because of You. You live in me
I live for You. You live through me. You give through me
Giving to others, my sisters and brothers. And to the lost
I give them You!

"For I am confident of this very thing, that He who began a good work in you will perfect it until the day of Jesus Christ."

(Phil. 1:6)

Tammy Jett

There is NO other God, then You!

"...Out of the mouths of babes and sucklings thou hast perfected praise?" (Mat. 21:16)

"I press on to reach the end of the race and receive the heavenly prize for which God, through Christ Jesus, is calling us." (Phil. 3:14)

"Set your mind on things above, not on earthly things." (Col. 3:2)

> *"...in this world we are like Jesus."*
> *(1 John 4:17)*

"...the lamb of God who takes away the sin of the world." (John 1:29)

"Trust in the Lord always and lean not on your own understanding." (Pro. 3:5)

"...I will send you an Advocate—the Spirit of truth. He will come to you from the Father and will testify all about me." (John 15-26)

Prayer

_____

_____

_____

_____

_____

_____

_____

_____

_____

Lord God, You Confound the Wise

Lord God, You take the foolish things
And confuse the wisest
Lord You are too funny
You take a sickling, with boils on his skin
Who's lost all family and all his friends
And You use him, to share perfect praise
You defeat the philistines, by a blind man
--By making him strong, in You again
You take the King, of all the world
Birth Him, among the farm animals
By a maiden, that's had no relations
You bring into the world, a Savior
Then a sinner, like Mary Magdalene
Is so loved and forgiven, anoints Him
Lord, you cause the lame to walk
The blind to see, the deaf to hear and talk
You take a Samaritan woman, at the well
Let her run, with the greatest news, to tell
You give, life changing words, in parables
And the worker, that comes in the evening
Gets the same pay, as the one there all day
Jesus, so different are your ways
Your thoughts are far, from ours
As far as, the heavens are from the earth
Your thoughts and ways, are far above ours

> "But God chose
> what is foolish in
> the world to shame
> the wise; God chose
> what
> is weak in the
> world to shame
> the strong."
>
> *(1 Cor. 1:27)*

> "As the heavens are
> higher than the
> earth, so are my
> ways higher than
> your ways and my
> thoughts than your
> thoughts."
> *(Is. 55:9)*

Father, I laugh at you and all the things you do! You are my only, "true!"
You take water and turn it to wine. use a donkey to speak, just in time
You feed multitudes from a, small lunch of fish. Tell fishermen, where to fish
And then, mold us, to become fishers of men. Jesus You confound the wise…

Lord, make us true, fishers of men!
Again

"Because we understand our fearful responsibility to the Lord, we work hard to persuade others."

"...Christ's love controls us. Since we believe that Christ died for all, we also believe that we have died to our old life. He died for everyone so that those who receive his new life will no longer live for themselves. Instead, they will live for Christ, who died and was raised for them.

So we have stopped evaluating others from a human point of view. How differently we know Him now! This means that anyone who belongs to Christ has become a new person. **The old life is gone; a new life has begun!**

And all of this is a gift from God, who brought us back to himself through Christ. And God has given us the task of reconciling people to Him. For God was in Christ, reconciling the world to Himself, no longer counting people's sin against them. And He gave us the wonderful message of reconciliation. So we are Christ's ambassadors; God is making His appeal through us. **We speak for Christ when we plead, "Come back to God!"** *For God made Christ, who never sinned, to be the offering for our sin, so that we could be made right with God through Christ." (2 Cor. 5:11-21)*

Prayer;

_____
_____
_____
_____
_____
_____
_____
_____
_____

Our Perfect Praise

Jesus…

I serve you
I honor you
I will obey
I don't want, to hear you say…
"Depart from me, I never knew you
When I was hungry, you didn't feed me
Thirsty, you gave me nothing to drink
Naked, you didn't clothe me
I was a stranger, you didn't take me in
Sick and in prison, you didn't visit me"
Others are in need
And they need me
To bring them, to You
We will go
Lord Jesus
I will go
We will only, follow You
Finally, we are true
We will go
You sent us all
Every one of us
I'm ready…

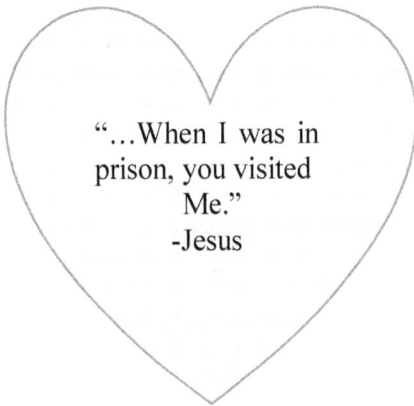

"…When I was in prison, you visited Me."
-Jesus

We are ready
To tell the world about you
Starting in our very own city, our neighborhoods
And also in the poverty stricken areas and in the prisons too
I Love You. We Love You. You asked us to go. We're gonna' listen
Lord we are gonna' be fishers of men, again! Amen

*"Because we understand our fearful responsibility to the Lord, **we work hard to persuade others.**" (2 Cor. 5:11)*

"Heal the sick, raise the dead...drive out demons. Freely you have received; freely give..." (Mat. 10:6)

"Go out to the highways and hedges and compel people to come in..." (Luke 14:23)

"...Paul devoted himself fully to the word, testifying to the Jews that Jesus is the Christ. But when they opposed and insulted him, he shook out his garments and told them, 'Your blood be on your own heads! I am innocent of it. From now on I will go to the Gentiles.' So Paul left the synagogue and went next door to the house of Titus Justus, a worshipper of God. Crispus, the synagogue leader, and his whole household believed in the Lord. And many of the Corinthians who heard the message believed and were baptized." (Acts 18: 5-8)

"One night the Lord spoke to Paul in a vision: 'Do not be afraid; keep on speaking, do not be silent.'" (Acts 18:9)

"Every day they continued to meet...ate together with glad and sincere hearts praising God...and the Lord added to their number daily those who were being saved. (Acts 2:46-47)

Prayer

_____
_____
_____
_____
_____
_____

CONCLUSION

My Story

Wolves and hirelings are everywhere
We, have not known how, to protect or care
We must now begin, to peg them, with a red flag
Jesus Christ says their purpose, is solely bad
I'm no longer nervous, no longer scared
After-all Jesus says, "they don't care."

A rapist is pegged for life. But a preacher
Just needs forgiveness, when he seduces your wife
Of course, we know, we all need to be, forgiven
But what about, when he continues that livin'?

Jesus says, "expel him from among you."
So he can repent and become brand new
But we say, "I love that preacher, when he preaches
I'm not worried about, what My father teaches"
We say, we are showing forgiveness and love
Yet, God's ways are under, and our ways above

Seems like Satan, all over again
Doesn't that Apple, look shiny and red
We act like young boys and girls
Testing the waters in this world
Yet, our Father knows our heart
He teaches us, to keep our lives, and sin apart

It's been, tormenting, over the years, speaking with no voice
Forever searching, for which words were the right choice
But now, finally, I'm free…
"My pastor seduced, my very best friends
Several years later, I climb out, of the pain within
I lost my sisters, my very best friends
As the church hid the sin within"

"My' pastor sent my family far away
So others would not, find out his ways
I was young, I was not strong
My family, spiraled down
I joined the Church, but I was *lost*, not found."

Satan took me on an emotional ride
The husbands of these friends, tried to call
I did not answer, as if to hide
I knew if they spoke to me, I would cry, the pain inside
So I never spoke, to my 'church' brothers and sisters again
Though, I loved them greatly. They were my best, friends

The new church, we were sent to, did not want our leadership
Because it was wrongly taken from another, which was our brother
So, now my new church family, split. Again many hurt
To cover, again, the pastor's dirt…whew! That's a lot of hurt
Where, oh where is the Church?

To the women, whom had these affairs
And all the others, out there
Our family, spiraled downward fast
Our youth, almost didn't last
Their entire quality of life changed
Coming from a place that caused much pain
Twenty years later, still paying the price
Of the pastor's demons, he chose to hide

These youth, no longer want to be in church
Help us Lord, to heal the hurt, through Your real work
Your works of love, in action, will show Your real love
The church we attended, though I thought, I loved
It was not love. It was lust. It was not real
Sin lived there, tore up families, everywhere

If the pastors, preachers, leaders and all…could
Just tell the many youth and families… Sorry
"Confess your faults, one to another." Help heal, others
No matter what we choose, pray to love and forgive
For we all have done wrong, in this life we live
I pray these pages have revealed, God's real work…
Because it's time for our cities, to experience, the 'real' church!

When the wickedness comes out of the church, you will deliver
The oppressed, the sick, the lame, the hurt!
"Judgement starts in the church."
These are God's words

His Glory

"We are the salt of the earth. If the salt has lost, its savor how can the earth be salted?" We are the light of the world? Do we light a candle to hide it under a bushel? Do we, "Let our light, so shine before men, that they may 'see' our good works and glorify our Father which is in heaven?" Where, is our "good work" in the neighborhood? Doesn't Jesus say, "Faith without works is dead faith?" So, would you agree, that praying for the neighborhoods and not 'going' to the neighborhoods, is dead faith?

We are doing our families and our cities a huge injustice by not exposing the wolves. Jesus, gave us these instructions, so we could protect one another, not that we would, tear anyone down. Our instructions from God are in place, to save our lives. Instead, often we choose, that many, would lose their lives. Mostly, this happens because of ignorance. Lack of the truth. But see that's the thing, a wolf will not teach, the whole truth. It's up to you! You've got to read and study.

Jesus is Not 'cool' with sin, living, in the Church. Wolves teach half- truths. Some, may teach, "we are forgiven." This is true. However, the other part of this truth is, "Shall we continue in sin…? God forbid. How shall we that are dead to sin live any longer in it?" (Rom. 6:1)

We will still make mistakes, but it's time to set the record straight. It's time for the 'real' church to go into the highways regularly and spread the true love of Jesus Christ. No longer 'covering' for the wolves that teach half-truths and refuse to go into the neighborhoods, into the prisons, and keep the worship facilities closed all week, and never bring in the homeless and the weak.

Church Facilities led by pastors that only mentor their own church member's youth, are wolves, hirelings. It is impossible to work, "for Jesus", living off of his tithe and offering, and not do the work He says do. Jesus is not going to give a pastor some famous purpose and contradict God's own words, we each have heard.

Prison Ministry. Homeless work. Highways and byways, the streets near your facility, is not optional. Think about it. If it were optional, forty-eight, out of fifty pastors in a small radius could decide 'their' ministry is to paint the sidewalks- So who would visit the prisoners and take care of the homeless and orphans. Largely we have a huge problem, because this is exactly what is happening. The pastors are leaving the 'massive' highways and byways ministry, prison ministry, homeless ministry, at-risk youth ministry to, no one. I don't know about you, but I hear Jesus loud and clear! "You, have turned My Father's house into a den of thieves…" (Mat. 21:13) - (Jere. 7:11)

Read the scriptures concerning, outreach. See if you think it's ok with Jesus to Live and go to church within twenty minutes from hopeless, lost, dying gang members, but "oh yeah, we drop off cake patties to the community yard sale. Oh, and we assist with all the events of the upcoming business owners of tomorrow, conference." Remember, Jesus says, "…I hold this against you, that you have abandoned the love you had at first. Remember therefore from where you have fallen; repent, and do the works you did at first. If not, I will come to you and remove your lampstand…" (Rev. 2:4)

Evaluate your church lifestyle, by the words of Christ. If your pastor is not involved in the assignments of Christ, Jesus says to, Flee. My sheep know My voice and a stranger they will not follow, they will, flee…" (John 10:5)

As God's children, we should know, without a doubt, our cities would experience a major revival and lives would be saved and changed in the neighborhoods and on the street, if we went into the highways… Jesus' words are true. Do we believe His word, any longer? The hirelings have us weak. Because they get paid, *not* going to the street. They are stealing God's pay! The pay intended to reach the lost, and build the city. The City of souls. The harvest is ready, Go! If you present to your pastor, a 'real' ministry. A chance to change lives massively, and he looks at you sideways and takes a deep breath or better yet, you never hear back, you can believe you are serving a hireling.

A person on fire for God never turns down a legit plan, to win lost souls. Remember we are like Christ, it's embedded in us to save lives. It's like a 'high' being on fire for Jesus Christ. It wakes us up at night. I couldn't sleep the other night, cryin' for the streets, plight. Went out to the street, got out of my car. Told the young woman, God sent me to where you are. I told her about the love of God. She told me her name. As we held hands and began to pray, she began to cry, then she spoke. She told me there was a man inside. Then 'he' asked me to pray, using his birth name.

**We're sitting around in our Churches lookin' cute, God's tryin'
to save the entire city, through you!**

Don't we believe His word, anymore?

- We overcome evil with good. This good is a verb.
- Greater is He that is within me, than he that is in this world."
- The name of the Lord is a strong tower, the righteous run in and are safe."

- If two or three gather in my name, there I am in the mist.
- If you ask anything in my name, I will do it!
- You will cast out demons in my name. – Jesus
- The harvest of souls is plentiful, but the laborers are few
- Depart from me, I never knew you, when I was hungry you did not feed me, thirsty, you gave me nothing to drink. A stranger and you did not take me in. Sick and in prison and you did not visit me.
- When the godly are in authority, the people rejoice, but when the wicked are in power, they groan.
 - You are the light of the world., a city on a hill
- Go to the highways and byways and compel others
- Heal the sick, raise the dead…drive out demons…

Do all I have said - Jesus

And Remember…

- Jesus

ACKNOWLEDGMENTS

To my Lord and Savior, Jesus Christ. Thank you, for giving new friends, the readers - insight, and having us 'feel' the heart of the fight, the struggle on the street, for the hurting and weak. - Out of all the times I have failed, I now represent You, well.

To my cousin, Wayne Quarles; you are a light in our big beautiful family. Thank you for your closeness to Christ and letting His light shine so bright in you, for all the world to see! Please let us know when you will be 'preaching.' Smile. 'We love you!

And...
To 'Our' Eldest brother, Elder Ricky Duffy, better known as, "Tuff Duff."
You have truly represented Christ well, my brother. Your integrity and loyalty to Christ, has been an amazement to me. I for one, see your sold out dedication, never wavering and ready to give a word at any and every given moment. You, totally keep me laughing. Never, ever can you ever be accused of being "lukewarm." Thank you for your unwavering, sold-out disposition and every moment lifestyle, for Christ. It has truly helped to redeem me. Thank you for showing me, Jesus and His love for me at all times. I honor you. I will always remember the day you pulled up and your tint on the "front" window said, "It's All About Jesus." Truly, I have never, in nearly 40 years, ever known it to be about anything else, with you. Wiping my tears now, I say Thank you, Thank you. Truly, I have found that love, that fire, that excitement for Jesus Christ, the every, breath, and heart -beat of my life! Ethel "Ruby" Duffy, girl I just shake my head. Amazing Jesus. Thank you sis, Thank you. Your wisdom has been with me through my every heartache. Thank you for being the Jesus, the bible, some may never read. I cherish and honor you, sis. Thank you.
Ricky Jr, Raquel, RaShaun and all the children– Love you, always.

"It's All About Jesus Ministries" – Cantonment, Florida
Elder and Sister Ricky Duffy
&
Family

ABOUT THE AUTHOR

Known as the "Outreach Coordinator" Angela Tanner, is a community youth, Magnet. When she goes into the neighborhoods, hundreds of kids are drawn. The parents and elderly soon fall in. – "Ms. Angela is an institution." – Chattanooga Free Press. She carries the simple message of God's love, with crafts and/or just good conversation. Often asked how she does this. She responds, "With love and kindness have I drawn thee. God's love is Mighty! Power to change a family, a community, an entire city. Jesus meant for us to change the world with His love!" Angela is an advocate for inner city, at risk youth, the hopeless, the less fortunate, the weak. Her organization, appeals to the Local Church to adopt the areas neighborhoods. She whole heartedly, believes, - "We overcome the magnitude of evil in our cities, with good, only by personally spreading God's love, through a written, committed plan, of His true works, carried out every day!" Acts 2:47 --Satan cannot stand, he cannot destroy, with the *real* Church, doing God's *real* work!
-- Jesus Christ Reigns!
Angela lives in Chattanooga, Tn. - Four of her children, also reside in "Chatt."
Angela has a vision for Jesus Christ to Reign over crime in Chattanooga
And all, heavy crime related cities. The '*real*' Church, is the Answer!

"Every City needs a Joseph." - Angela
(Genesis 39:3-5)

Angela D. Tanner
www.ChatttownMissions.com.
Angela@ChatttownMissions.com
- Chatttown Missions, The Magnet Church - "We are fishers of men"

PRAYER

Dear Lord, the one reading this has a specific plan from you. But Lord never again let this sister or brother forget your main plan. Your main purpose for coming, to die for our sins, that all may be born again! Lord may they not rest from your fire, Lord! May each person in their neighborhood accept you, Jesus as their Lord and Savior, through a committed plan of prayer and outreach. Then Lord have this one, begin to organize prison ministry and reach the city with the plan, that comes from your Miraculous, Holy, Powerful hand! Lord. Fill this one with your joy, wisdom and power, to live holy and do your greater works.
Amen!

"Now go and do as He really did." - Love Angela

www.ingramcontent.com/pod-product-compliance
Lightning Source LLC
LaVergne TN
LVHW081327060426
835513LV00012B/1212